CW00690265

LOCHORE

AN AUTHORISED BIOGRAPHY

LOCHORE

AN AUTHORISED BIOGRAPHY

ALEX VEYSEY, GARY CAFFELL, RON PALENSKI

Hodder Moa Beckett

ISBN 1-86958-303-5

Published in 1996 by Hodder Moa Beckett Publishers Limited
(a member of the Hodder Headline Group)
4 Whetu Place, Mairangi Bay, Auckland, New Zealand

Cover Photos: Andrew Cornaga (front) & Peter Bush (back)

Typeset by: TTS Jazz, Auckland

Printed through Colorcraft Ltd, Hong Kong

CONTENTS

ACKNOWLEDGEMENTS

Thanks to friends and colleagues: Alex Veysey, Gary Caffell and Ron Palenski; Fred Allen, Charlie Saxton, Peter Bush, Sean Fitzpatrick, Colin Meads, Earle Kirton and Laurie Mains. Special thanks also to Pam and my family.

Brian Lochore

FOREWORD

I am honoured to write this foreword to the story of a man who occupies such a lofty pedestal in rugby history. I have long been an admirer and supporter of the splendid qualities shown by Brian Lochore, both as a man and player. When I first met him I perceived in him a downright honesty and sincerity. These stem from his being a typical New Zealand farmer, a man of the land, straight up and down, hard, strong and very physical.

I was fully aware of the controversy that would ensue when I was the principal architect in appointing Brian captain of the 1966 All Blacks to replace the retiring Wilson Whineray. I think BJ was, perhaps, the most surprised of all. He was chosen ahead of greats such as Meads, Tremain, Graham, Gray, Laidlaw and MacRae. History has proved it was the right decision because in the years that followed he turned up absolute trumps, first as an All Black captain, and then as the All Black coach. This man had the mana that comes with respect, with looking people in the eye. He was warm and understanding, but brooked no nonsense. He played fair and clean, and always by the book.

As the new captain Brian made a spectacular start. In a clean sweep the British Isles were beaten four-nil. Success continued in 1967 when the Wallabies were easily beaten. Then followed England, Wales, France and Scotland. As success followed success Brian was an inspiration, constantly proving himself as an intelligent, thinking footballer with wonderful anticipation and ball-handling skills.

This dignified man was a management's dream. His fair-mindedness, his judgement and his discipline, both on and off the field, have seldom been equalled. I admire him for the wonderful family man he has always been with his super wife Pam, who gave him the total support so necessary for him to succeed, a support I so readily recognised because I received it from my own wife Norma.

Brian has never lost touch. He helped to select and coach the great All Black sides of the 1980s and he again soared to another sporting pinnacle when he coached the 1987 All Blacks to their famous inaugural World Cup victory.

Today Brian Lochore is still the same softly spoken, gentlemanly, rather shy person he has always been. In spite of all the glory he has achieved nothing has changed. Together, for quite a period, we experienced sporting success at its sublime best. Memories of those days and the memory of my association with this remarkable man will always remain with me.

Fred R Allen

Fred Allen
April 1996

FOREWORD

When the so-called Baby Blacks were selected to play France in 1986 the trepidation was not all out there among supporters of the game who feared for the fate of these untried tyros of international rugby. As players we had trepidation enough for the whole country.

The circumstances were unique – selected to represent New Zealand against a famously difficult opponent in the absence through suspension of a great proportion of the country's top players. Other than by the players, it can never accurately be measured or appreciated what Brian Lochore meant in the presentation of those young, even naive, players as a team which would beat France. The night before the test he spoke to us quietly from the heart. It was motivation taken out of the common ruck of bombast and hype. It encompassed his understanding of our concerns and his belief that we were players and men enough to represent New Zealand with the sort of pride which overcomes many perceived handicaps.

That night BJ won friends for life. It was no act. It was Lochore being Lochore. I had experienced much the same sort of quiet sincerity two years before when he selected me in the New Zealand Colts team and I was to experience it often during the 1987 World Cup campaign and again when he was a huge influence before and during the 1995 campaign. Beyond anyone else, he was able to make the players understand what being an All Black meant, not just by the words he chose but by a physical presence which rested as much on his dignity and sincerity as on his size.

As captain of the All Blacks in 1995 I turned to him as some sort of father-figure. As one of the great All Black captains he was quick to understand and problems, under his scrutiny and advice, diminished. He inspired trust. It is not always easy for men of one generation to inspire unswerving loyalty from those of a later one, but BJ held the All Blacks who came under his influence in the palm of his hand.

He had, too, the natural sensitivity to draw our families into the circle, to have them feel rugby and, more particularly, our careers in it were not isolated from them. This has created a warmer, more embracing sense of team than was experienced by All Blacks of earlier vintages.

It is important to rugby and to people's perception of it that BJ's life and times should now be recorded. I am honoured to be a part of this book.

Sean Fitzpatrick

Sean Fitzpatrick
April 1996

INTRODUCTION

For thirty years or so, from time to time people suggested to me that I should write a book. Some of the suggestions were from friends, some from journalists and some from publishers. My immediate reaction to all of those suggestions was: "Why?"

I'd always felt uncomfortable with the idea, and I just had no desire to put my thoughts on paper. The matches in which I'd played were all covered to one extent or another in books and I didn't see any point in adding my own views.

Things change, of course. If it was just my playing career, I'd still be saying no. But over the last few years the suggestions have arisen again and people have said I ought to write a book because I have been involved in some significant happenings in New Zealand rugby, such as the World Cups in 1987 and '95 and the negotiations over contracts with players, and I owed it to history to put these things down.

Well, I've never been in debt to history before and I thought these people probably had a point. So I agreed on a book not so much for me, but for posterity, so the events of those years are down on paper, through the eyes of one man who was involved.

Agreeing to a book is one thing, getting it done is another.

My career in rugby has been in three distinct parts – as an All Black through the sixties, as a player and coach in Wairarapa that became Wairarapa-Bush, and as a coach and a sort of odd-jobs man at the national level. I decided to ask for help from three writers most involved in each of these phases.

Alex Veysey covered rugby for *The Dominion* and the *Sunday Times* during my playing career, he went on the long tour of Britain and France with the All Blacks in 1963-64, I had always admired his work and got on well with him personally. Gary Caffell lives in Masterton and works for the *Wairarapa Times-*

Age and was ideal to write about that period of my life when I coached Wairarapa-Bush. Ron Palenski covered the first World Cup in 1987 for *The Dominion* and a lot of other rugby besides and has a sound knowledge of rugby events.

It might be unusual for a book to have three authors, but it seemed a convenient way of handling it and I thank each of them for their help and input.

For me, rugby is the ultimate in team games and anything any one player achieves is a result, directly or indirectly, of the work and help of others. I have had much assistance during my various rugby careers.

Fred Allen was coach while I was captain of the All Blacks and he had a huge influence on me then and later. During my coaching, I tried to emulate Fred in some of the ways he went about presenting and motivating teams – though I don't think I was ever The Needle!

The New Zealand Rugby Union has had some fine administrators with whom I've worked. They've been men of integrity, intelligence and substance and I owe them all my thanks.

Rugby is like a freemasonry and there are people who have given me all manner of assistance over the years. I could never attempt to isolate or name them, but I would like to thank the people at the Masterton club who were of such assistance to me in many ways, but especially going out and keeping the farm ticking over while I was away.

The biggest debt of gratitude is due to my family. My wife Pam and children Sandra, Joanne and David have been totally supportive in everything I've done or tried to do and nothing could have happened without them. They have been my props.

And thanks must also go to Pam and my immediate families for their help and for just being there.

Brian Lochore

Brian Lochore
April 1996

PART ONE
ALEX VEYSEY

1
PIONEER IN SPIRIT

Had he the choice, Brian James Lochore would have been a child of the 1870s and a young farmer of the 1890s, a pioneer breaking in the land with horse and plough, responding to challenge as it does not exist in the age of machine and high technology in agriculture. And if that meant being a 1905 All Black, that would have been just fine with him too.

Pioneering in farming and rugby would have suited him. Men survived on their will, their heart for the contest and on their skill and capacity to make things happen. They were good at what they did or they could not last. Come flood or drought, survival was still in their own hands and minds. Reputation was nothing, deeds everything. Relationships were communal and close. Beyond all, life was a challenge.

Instinctive response to challenge was bred into Brian Lochore. It was in his childish curiosity and experimentation on the family farm. It was in his testing of the adult system, his adventuring with the patience of his elders. He detected challenge in most things and in nothing more than the implication that there were things his father could do which he could not. Almost by the day he bore evidence that the consequences of taking up what he saw as challenges or adventures were more painful than rewarding. If he did not get a hiding a day it had been a pretty boring 24 hours.

Inevitably, farming was to be his life from the time his father, Jim Lochore, married Alma Joyce Wyeth, a 5ft 1in package of the same resolution with which her grandfather, Thomas Wyeth, had pioneered farming in the Wairarapa and with which his father, Robert, had broken in land in Upper Hutt and Stokes Valley. Robert, a timber-feller, had come to New Zealand in the New Zealand Company barque *Cuba* in 1839, hired as a labourer to join the surveying staff of Colonel William Wakefield at Port Nicholson.

Thomas and his brother Charles, both champion athletes, helped construct the first telegraph line from Wellington to Masterton about 1867, horse-carting the materials, clearing the bush, hewing the posts, erecting them and laying line from ridge to ridge across the jagged terrain of the Rimutakas. He helped, too, in the clearance of Rimutaka bush for the Upper Hutt - Featherston stretch of the Wellington-Wairarapa railway. And it was in the Wairarapa that the Wyeths planted their roots and farmed the land.

But it was at a whim of Nature long before that the Wyeths became the Wairarapa Wyeths, that Jim Lochore ever met Joyce and that Brian Lochore became the Lochore of Wairarapa. During 1848, floods and earthquakes devastated the plans and hopes of pioneers in the Wellington area. In October many settlers, the Wyeths and their closest friends, the Sykeses, among them, boarded the barque *Subraon* to go home to England via Australia. Off Seatoun, in gathering darkness and in a heavy swell and rising southerly, the barque struck an uncharted rock, lost her rudder and took water fast. From a terrifying situation threatening tragedy all were saved. At the height of the storm, when all seemed lost, the matriarch of the Sykeses, a deeply religious woman, swore she heard the voice of God saying, as it had to Peter as he fled the vengeance of the Romans, "Quo vadis? Whither goest thou?" Thus, she said, it was ordained that they were not to leave New Zealand . . . "we were to go on shore and start life again with patience and fortitude". Which, of course, they did.

When Brian Lochore talks of the rugby in Scotland it is with something approaching family affection. "They are us," he says, "they are us. Going to Scotland is like being home." The first

16

New Zealand Lochore, Robert, son of a Stirlingshire minister, effectively wrote his name into the pioneering folklore of the South Island. A considerable academic, he found the mercantile life which followed study neither remunerative nor congenial. With his brother James he sailed for Port Phillip. He worked on cattle and sheep stations along the Murray River, became a skilled horseman and bushman, took his place without measurable reward in the Bendigo gold rush of 1851 and in 1857 came to Port Chalmers in the brig *Thompson and Henry*, chartered to bring sheep to stock new country bordering Southland and Otago.

Restlessly, he explored great tracts of country on foot, came to know Gabriel Reid and was one of the first twenty prospectors into Gabriel's Gully. Given a nod and a wink by Reid he and his small party took a thousand pounds' worth of gold in three months but in forty years of self-imposed slavery to hope, mining mostly in Liverpool Bill's Gully on the West Coast, he unearthed no comparable bonanzas.

It was Robert's great-grandson, George, who took the Lochore name to the Wairarapa, to Masterton, where Brian's father was born, educated, married and sired one of New Zealand's greatest All Black captains.

Understanding the pioneering fortitude of the Wyeths and the Lochores is crucial to understanding Brian Lochore. What has driven him as farmer and rugby player and captain are largely the same qualities which encouraged pioneers to persevere through adversities we cannot begin to comprehend – resolution, stamina, integrity, a rugged dignity and an inborn sense of respect for and duty to others.

Not that as a growing boy Lochore could care less about chasing a rugby ball around the paddocks. He set his heart on becoming a jockey. His love of horses was without reservation. The regularity with which at first he fell from them, diminished neither his affection for them nor his determination to stay on them. He trusted implicitly his grandfather's advice that he could not be a good rider unless he fell off twenty times and that after the twentieth fall the horse would tire of the sport. Were that the price to be paid for becoming a jockey it was fine by the boy. His first horse was a jet-black Shetland named Winkle which, he was long convinced, came down the chimney on Christmas Day, 1943, when he was three. He knew it came down the chimney because there were the unmistakable signs and smells of a healthy horse all the way down the passage leading to Winkle under the tree . . .

"Winkle had never been advised of my grandfather's philosophy. He never tired of the sport. When I had fallen from him twenty times it was merely time for the second half. He was quiet enough but with a hard core of cunning. While you conformed to the standards he set he was co-operative. But he could drop you with a twitch if you tried to get smart. He was versatile, too. If I was being altogether too smart he would shoot under the trees and let the branches wipe me off, which was pretty undignified even for a three-and four-year-old. Or he'd trot along amiably enough and stop dead, shoot me over his neck and eat grass before I hit the deck.

"Winkle designated saddle-days and no-saddle days. He had us flummoxed by his ability to shed a saddle. He blew out his stomach, turned his head and watched Dad tie the girth as tight as he could. Then he'd relax and Dad, wise to that game, tightened the girth further. Winkle patiently went through the process again until Dad swore the girth was immovable. But it was nothing more than another challenge. Winkle put his head down between his knees, wriggled his shoulders, stepped out of the saddle and ate some more grass.

"Those were quite harsh days financially on the farm. There was no way we could afford a horse-float but my mother and father wanted me to have the chance of riding-tuition a pony club would give me. The Solway Showgrounds were too distant to ride to so Dad came up with an answer so simple it took my breath away. He would put Winkle in the back of the car and drive him. It took some sort of man to put his son's pony in the family Chevvy and arrive at gymkhanas where most of the horse-floats were a lot flasher than our car. And it took some sort of concentration on the road by other drivers as we passed with Winkle's head out the window taking the breeze."

The little Shetland pony was the beginning of a life-long love affair with horses. Brian rode along for hours in the furrows behind his father's horse-drawn plough, dreaming of jockeys' silks and the thrill of the race and flashing past the post after a brilliant ride. The Lochore farm was neighbour to the Opaki racecourse, a substantial training establishment. He went to primary school with Bubs and Gary Jenkins who, as part of the well-known racing family, were to become top jockeys. They filled his head with stories of racetrack and stables. His tutor at the pony club was Nancy Williams who, with her husband Alister, founded one of Australasia's most renowned and most beautiful thoroughbred breeding properties, Te Parae, home of the matchless broodmare Sunbride and the supreme sire Oncidium.

When Brian grew out of Winkle – and almost simultaneously started reaching beyond acceptable jockey-size – the tiny horse, with his almost-lovable mix of cunning and wisdom, taught virtually the whole district to ride. Brian was by then sufficiently accomplished to be given the rougher horses around the district, gentling them for other children. He felt fear for no horse. What he did feel and what he trusted was rapport which seemed to inspire swift understanding from the most fickle-tempered of them. He never lost the touch, much preferred to ride horses around his own hilly farm and, while recognising the inevitability of motor-driven wheels, somehow resented their invasion.

There is still a yearning in him for the days when horses were everything to farmers. "To be 20 in the 1890s . . . oh boy, that was my style, my pace. That was my sort of challenge." And as he speaks, he hears the ripping snort of a farm-bike out on the hills, puts his hand over his eyes and adds, "I'm not a modern person. I wish . . . I wish we were still ploughing with horses; we were manual farmers. It may be that pre-hitech age in which I was brought up to farm produced that last generation of genuine 'old-fashioned' farmers which made of All Blacks naturally hard, fit men."

He has bred and raced winning horses but is not much of a punter. Race days for him are not dollar-days. They are days still to wonder at the beauty of the animals and to become lost in the thrill of the contest as the horses stretch out and surge to the post for within them there is more than beauty. There is courage.

Every family needs a dynamo and to the Lochore family Joyce, the Wyeth, was it. She was a muscly go-getter – "a little Sherman tank," Brian calls her – a practical farming woman, forced out of boarding school and back to the family farm by the depression. She was a spinner, a knitter, an extra hand in every aspect of farming husbandry, the daughter of farmers, the grand-daughter of farmers, the sister of farmers and the fount of farming knowledge from which Jim Lochore drew strength and his own knowledge.

Before rugby meant anything at all to Brian, even while Winkle filled his days, he had a tennis racquet thrust into his hands and it was from that beginning that tennis became his first sporting love. The local tennis club was the pikelets-scones-and-tea hub of all social life and it was where the Lochores spent much of their hard-earned leisure time. Jim was a good natural sportsman. Joyce was all flat-out determination; no great stylist but with the priceless quality of fighting for every point. The combination of Jim's natural skill and Joyce's tenacity gave their three sons and daughter better than a starter's chance.

Brian, the eldest, became a highly ranked age-group tennis player and the top player in his province. Kevin was a good all-rounder with fine hand-eye co-ordination whether at tennis, hockey or rugby – at which he locked the Masterton junior scrum with a tall youngster named Richard Collinge, who was to become a left-arm quick bowler of world class. The youngest brother, Wayne, had such natural sporting talent and such versatility that he might have gone to the very top whether in tennis, rugby or track. "Such talent, such mind-blowing talent," Brian reflects. "Maybe it's better not to have all that talent, better to know you have to work to achieve. I was blessed with some ability but not so much that I didn't have to work to improve. Had I the talent of Wayne I might not have been the rugby player I became. Other than at tennis I didn't really rank at college. He was a goal-kicking first five-eighth, top of the tennis team, track champion, nationally ranked as an under-16 and under-18 tennis player. Me? I won the half-mile walk which seemed at that stage of my development to be a pretty attractive pursuit."

Wayne's twin, Shona, turned to tramping with great enthusiasm.

Rugby was always thereabouts, just as it is in every New Zealand rural community, and as a primary schoolboy Brian was called into the Wairarapa trials. In an hour of football he never once touched the ball. It was either tantalisingly close or measureless miles away in someone else's hands or on the end of someone else's boot. About the same time all over the country small boys were chasing in frustration or mystification a vexatiously designed ball which bounced all over the place in a manner real, round balls did not.

"The game was such a bloody mystery to most little kids," says Brian. "As a country schoolboy I was naturally shy. There were some very good footy players who tended to dominate the action while I hovered. Hovering paid off. I got in the primary school reps and to this day I do not understand why unless in those days chasing without touching was seen to be a desirable quality in a budding footballer. I think I got a sympathy vote for fruitless persistence."

The other quality which probably attracted the admiration of the selectors was that he wore headgear. He was not sure why except that his All Black idol, Tiny White, wore headgear and if it was good enough for Tiny White it was good enough for him. He would not be the first player – and even in considerably higher echelons of the game – who, in a close call, has won the selectors' nod because his headgear made him fractionally more memorable.

Rugby was beginning to nudge at tennis. In his third year at Wairarapa College he made the First XV as a flanker and on Saturday, September 1, 1956, as he was put on a train in Auckland to return home from a national tennis coaching school, he was very conscious that Robin Archer was about to kick off against the Springboks at Eden Park and that Tiny White, headgear rampant, would be leaping to attack the kick-off. Even as a teenager he was spellbound by the unfolding drama of the Springbok tour of 1956, caught up in the epidemic which swept the country into a nationalistic fervour not seen before or since. He remembers the almost hysterical anticipation of test matches not merely as games of rugby but as gladiatorial battles in which the good guys were dressed in black. And he regrets that as test matches have become commonplace the atmosphere of the occasion has drifted into the commonplace with them.

"Something which spelled rugby has gone . . . the overnight sleepouts which meant the contest for the best places on the embankment was really on; the window displays, the parades, the mad excitement which turned cities, towns and villages upside-down in anticipation of the test match. Rugby is becoming more the game for those who can afford reserved seats. The two-bob seats for the overnight sleeping-bag brigade are phased out in favour of corporate boxes often filled with people to whom the social small-talk is more important than the spectacle on the field. I know corporate money is crucial to the game as it has evolved into professionalism and that it would be naive to expect all the old character and characters of rugby to flow through that process but I do feel a sense of loss as test matches lose that quality of rarity which made them the jewels in rugby's crown."

Lochore describes himself as a "sports student" at college. His prime subject was agriculture but in most subjects his reports were of the "could do better" sort familiar to hundreds of thousands of parents coming to terms at last with the awful truth that they have not, after all, bred a brain surgeon. Getting into the First XV was a greater distinction by far than weaving through the intricacies of English syntax and analysis but it was not until he was in his last year of college that the team structure of rugby became as appealing to him as the individuality of tennis. He did not desert tennis. He found he could succeed well enough playing both sports for a time. He and his partner won the Wairarapa open doubles twice before he became an All Black and then he did not play a game of tennis for seven years. He could not afford to. Summer became the farming catch-up season after playing an increasingly demanding winter of rugby.

Lochore's farming life really started from the day he was born. It is in the nature of farming that families farm, not just fathers. Growing up was practical farming experience because it was always there; chores were farm chores; he saw ewes served and lambs born. The college agriculture course in theory and practice was, in effect, his finishing school. From college he went on to the family farm, learned to shear and, in travelling to shear at other properties, learned more of farming. When he was 16 he started his first day of shearing at 5.30 in the morning and 86 shorn-sheep later knew that total physical exhaustion did not mean raising a sweat in a college rugby match. The next day he sheared 94, the next 100.

"Shearing is challenge. You learn a lot about yourself. You are pitting yourself against yourself from day to day. I came to love shearing for the challenge and for the exhaustion at the end of the day. If you don't believe utter exhaustion can bring with it an almost overwhelming sense of fulfilment, of something approaching euphoria, you haven't sheared, you haven't played test rugby – you haven't lived."

On reflection, he regrets that rather than going from college on to the family farm he did not search out experience on one of the magnificent high-country stations of the South Island. There is something there, he believes, of matchless challenge for a farmer, something of vibrance, an environment to lift the soul. His regret is that he did not take up that challenge and turn it into a priceless experience.

Rugby coaching at Wairarapa College was much more structured and authoritative than at many country schools. Lochore's first coach for both tennis and rugby was Les Ingham who, with Ivan Dale, one of the Wairarapa players who lifted the Ranfurly Shield from Canterbury in 1950, gave him the ground rules. In the First XV he was coached by Gordon Henderson, a North Island representative as a loose forward in 1948 and New Zealand reserve in 1949.

"Through these men I was pulled into an understanding that rugby was not just a game where you chased the ball and hoped to get your hands on it from time to time; that it was a game of planning in which without the player-techniques and skills the planning went for nothing. As I grew to understand the structure of the game I was more and more absorbed by its reliance on teamwork with player working for player, a mutual reliance which placed team before individual."

As a 17-year-old and a regular junior player for the Masterton club he experienced senior rugby for the first time. In the dressing shed after playing in a curtain-raiser to the senior match he was counteracting the loss of body-fluid with a medication which, he being only 17, could not possibly have been Tui draught from the "home" brewery up the road in Eketahuna. Someone said, "Hey, you, go easy. You're standing by for the seniors." He stood by for the first half, went on in the second and when the ball was kicked far downfield he loped after it at Masterton junior pace. The captain, "Bottle" Hayward, a prop, steamed past him yelling, "In this team, son, you bloody-well *run*." It was, says Lochore, a message which made a lasting impression. He was never again overtaken by a prop.

Rustic communities seem much more readily than suburbia to throw up singular characters for the rest of the world to delight in. "Bottle" Hayward was one of those. On match day he arrived with a sack over his shoulder. He upended this in the middle of the floor and from it tumbled and clattered seven boots bearing the mud of several training runs and a couple of matches, four jerseys and five pairs of shorts, similarly decorated, three and a half jockstraps, of unspeakable vintage, and eleven socks, much favoured by the family moths. "Bottle" studied the steaming pile with great interest while rubbing his jaw, then, with almost feminine delicacy, selected his garments for the day's match which, invariably, he played loudly and with great concentration on the game's most basic basics.

Those were the days when rugby was everything to rural communities. It bound the people together. It made neither judgements nor distinctions. It created no divisions. It was the game for all the people. It brought town and country together as a community more warmly than any other activity. Farmers, freezing workers, lawyers, accountants, shearers and grocers . . . rugby was the great leveller. "Rugby means much more to New Zealand than test matches lost or won and much more than the fleeting careers of its superstars. Historically, it has been at the core of community togetherness and advancement. People have become more critical, more questioning of events in rugby. That's healthy, too. When I listen to rugby talkback on radio I'm sure we're in danger of becoming a nation of grizzlers. But the truth of rugby as the binding culture of the people has not changed."

Lochore's first full season of senior rugby in 1959 was also his first season of representative rugby. It was his introduction to a singular breed of rugby men who were to play a telling role in his career. His captain was Alan ("Kiwi") Blake, who was one of the deathless band of 2NZEF Army players known as the Kiwis, who with brilliance and daring resurrected rugby in post-war Britain and to a very significant extent in post-war New Zealand.

Blake in 1959 was 37 years old and had played 167 first class games, one of them a test in 1949. Wairarapa teams seemed year by year by year to be wrapped around the name of "Kiwi" Blake and many young players who passed through his hands retired long before he did while knowing a great deal more about the arts and artifices of lineouts than when they began.

To young Lochore, Blake was a sort of rugby father-figure, one who had been playing for Wairarapa just about for ever. He had played his first game for the province in 1941 as a lean, loose-limbed forward and by 1959, long converted to lock, was still as lean and by now more the spiritual leader than the rakish loosie at the head of the pack. But under his guidance the Wairarapa-Bush forwards interfered precociously for a time with the lineout drills of the 1959 Lions and with disconcerting ferocity tore into their work.

Before selection in the Wairarapa-Bush team Lochore played in a series of trials. For a brief time he found trial rugby as mystifying as he had found the game as a primary schoolboy. He learned the harsh fact of life that in a trial such idealistic perceptions of rugby as the ultimate team game were for the wet-behind-the-ears and that self-preservation, even from one's own teammates, was paramount. There was little in the way of pre-planned lineout calls and in the dog-eat-dog climate of the trial the young Lochore found himself either being directed or physically shuffled further and further back by players deeply concerned that he was stealing a march at number two. He overcame the problem by sprinting madly to lineouts when the ball went into touch, taking up his position and then stoutly resisting all attempts to shovel him to the rear.

The Lions fielded a team of whom nine – six of them backs – were to play three days later in the third test. Lochore, aged 18, found the experience exhilarating and educational. The Lions' prime jumpers were Richard Marques, an Englishman about as tall as most buildings in Masterton but not as immovable, and Rhys Williams, one of the greatest of all Welsh players. In there with them were such shrewd Welsh heads as Ray Prosser and Brin Meredith – the very Meredith who was to be at the source of Lochore's despair following the 1963-64 All Blacks' loss to Newport. The loose forwards were the Scot Ken Smith, the young Welsh tearaway Haydn Morgan and Ned Ashcroft, of England. Smith, Williams and Morgan would play in the Saturday test.

Of the backs, only the experienced English centre Jeff Butterfield was not to play in the following test. This meant that the backblocks boys were required to hold in check a most brilliant band of players – Ken Scotland, Peter Jackson, David Hewitt, Butterfield, Tony O'Reilly, Phil Horrocks-Taylor and Dickie Jeeps.

For flanker Lochore at 18, the difficulty in preparing to play the 1959 Lions, at their best among the most brilliant attackers of all teams, was one of coming to terms with the reality of it. On the field the reality was swift of impact: Hewitt's silky incisions and timing of the pass; Jackson's sleight of hand and foot; the bruising physicality of contact-exchanges with international forwards. But once acclimatised Lochore thrived, won possession at the back of the lineout and was very much "in" the game as the Wairarapa-Bush forwards disconcerted the Lions. Among many tackles he made, one on Jackson saved a try and, overall, he so impressed the rugby writer Terry McLean that he identified Lochore as one of the most promising forwards to play against the Lions on the tour.

The Lions won the match 37-11, Lochore emerged from it with a deeper knowledge of himself as a player and, with it, greater confidence, with clearer understanding of the lines of defence and with his standing as a committed forager and tackler greatly enhanced. It was a game, too, in which the Wairarapa-Bush team suffered from the unfathomable logic of the International Rugby Board that within the pure-set boundaries of the amateur code there was no place for the replacement of injured players. First five-eighth Rikys suffered a severe ankle injury which effectively removed him from the game though he persisted as an extra back. This took the number eight, Keegan, out of the pack to play at centre. Midway through the second spell Kiwi Blake retired with a facial injury. Lochore remembers it wryly because in the first spell the Wairarapa-Bush forwards had been taking the game to the Lions with startling success.

"The no-replacement rule belonged somewhere in another civilisation. It called blindly on a man's courage and spirit not to let the side down, placing him at further risk and the likelihood that the injury would be aggravated. I know in some cases this resulted in long-term complications which dogged players throughout their lives. I remember as a kid seeing photographs of the New Zealand captain, Ron Elvidge, crashing over for a try against the 1950 Lions while severely injured about the head, chest and shoulder. It was hailed as a great feat of courage – and so it was – but it was also evidence that the no-replacement rule was a mindless aberration in the administration of the game. That test was the same one in which the New Zealand prop Johnny Simpson had to leave the field early with a shattered knee, forcing one of the loose forwards, Jack McNab, into the front row. When Elvidge was injured the number eight, Peter Johnstone, went to the backs and the All Blacks were left with a six-man scrum.

"This is sport we're talking about and, in those days, a sport the players played with no reward other than honour and broken bones. It was amateurism taken to irrational lengths. It was astonishing that after such events as the 1950 test the rule was not modified as a matter of urgency. However, I do believe we have now gone so far in the other direction that it, too, verges on the ridiculous."

Lochore's first impressions of trial rugby were not measurably changed after his second experience among players who, while far more elevated, pursued their ends with much the same down-to-earth philosophy of self-help at all costs. Called to the North Island trials of 1961 in Palmerston North, his anticipation that in this lofty company the organised team game would be paramount was quickly and rudely dissipated and he was as quick to enter into the prevalent musketeer-spirit of all for one provided the one was one's self.

When he arrived at the teams' hotel in his green Wairarapa blazer, gee-whiz, he was greeted by an affable Ian Clarke, long-established All Black, who said, "Gidday. You must be Brian Lochore. Come and meet these other jokers." To Lochore these other jokers were royalty in rugby terms – among them Wilson Whineray, Don Clarke, Des Connor, Nev MacEwan, Dick ("Red") Conway, Ross Brown. And as anonymously as Lochore, a Wellington prop named Ken Gray was there to have his first trial, but as a lock. At this time Lochore had some experience as a lock but was named in his more usual role as a flanker for the late trial. It may be the most unexpected statistic of Lochore's career that, in fact, he never played a game of rugby at number eight in any grade until his first game for the All Blacks against Oxford University in 1963.

Whineray led Lochore's team at the North Island trial but has no recollection of the player who five years later was to succeed him as captain of the All Blacks. Whineray's first memory of Lochore coincides with the first memory of the thousands who in 1963 at an Athletic Park trial heard the distinctively bucolic voice of a Wairarapa supporter incessantly, desperately, boomingly pleading with Lochore to "C'mon!" Lochore's recollection of the 1961 event is clear. It endorsed everything he had learned about trials in the Wairarapa.

By then he had come through his second year of representative rugby and had found that he had developed sufficient of a reputation to make his second year more difficult by far than his first.

"The first year is a piece of cake. You are unknown. You are not someone who can be planned for and knocked off his game. So you just get out there and go for it. To me that meant attacking the ball and using my skills. I was raw but I was fit. I didn't think much about the game other than to give it my best shot for eighty minutes. To be going as hard at the end of it as the beginning, to trust my stamina . . . I suppose that was my approach throughout my career. I had confidence in my body to go the full game at whatever pace it developed. Like most of the country players I ran the hills until it got too dark, then pounded the roads. I always knew I was as fit as anyone on the paddock.

"The second year you find a lot of players getting in your way. You play, say, Hawke's Bay, Wellington and Manawatu again and life is very much harder. You find you're getting knocked around, that there's no such thing as free passage to the ball and that when you jump in the lineout someone's boot is on your foot, someone's hand has got itself tangled in your shorts or someone's elbow has given you an affectionate nudge in the ribs. Being planned-for may be some sort of compliment but it makes life bloody hard for a lanky youth who thinks he has the game sussed. So, the second year was clearly my hardest. But you absorb the lessons and the next season you're harder in every sense. You're ready to compete rather than expecting it all to happen for you. That's when you become a rugby player.

"Rugby is a game you learn on your feet. Every game throws up a new circumstance, a new challenge. You work out how best to overcome an awkward opponent, how you may 'think' him out of the game because, for all its physical character, rugby is a thinking game. The street-smart player, the player who thinks better and longer than his opponent, will overcome and survive. Do you have dominance over him in the last fifteen minutes? If not, he's beaten you."

If you went to trials as a spectator in the 1960s you went either because you were a compulsive rugby nut or because you were a compulsive rugby optimist. It was rare for a trial to be anything but a sketchy, patternless non-event over which the selectors nodded their heads sagely and learned little, if anything, they did not already know. The preparation of the teams was little more than a shrug of compliance with the inevitability that the game would be as haphazard as last year's. Regrettably, the trials of 1961 were not to be among the exceptions and Lochore was quick to seize on the need to "personalise" his game.

"The coaches were pulled in from around the region and thrown in with players they did not know. Game plans were vague and, as the games meandered on, became vaguer. Players pushed their own barrows. A country boy like me could become isolated from one of his playing strengths, waiting for lineout throws which never came. Often, provincial allegiance dictated that a wing throwing the ball in would throw to his provincial jumpers. So for me it was to hell with plans and tactics. If this was to be cut-throat I could be as bloody as the next man. Every throw to the lineout was, potentially, a throw for me and if that meant plundering someone else's ball, so be it. It was open slather and you had to get your hands on more ball than the other guy whether he was opposition or teammate.

"Trial rugby might have been a joke to watch but it was deadly serious for the players. I ran all day but running defence lines or attacking lines were not priorities. I just went where I felt the ball was going to be. In that trial Red Conway was in the opposition and that made it difficult. In that and other trials I seemed all day to be tackling Conway because he was such a swift marauding player, so often first to the loose ball. He had that red-headed, hard-minded, body-on-the-line attitude of a lot of those great lightweight loosies. I had enormous respect for him although he was preventing me from doing all the things I needed to be doing. But Red was also my tutor in a way. He was telling me I had to get there quicker. I had to be street-smart. To me, being street-smart came with sharpened anticipation rather than from cutting corners. I was never much good at cutting corners. I wasn't a good enough cheat. To be a good cheat you have to work at it conscientiously, and I should know because I've played with and against both highly polished ones and some bull-headed ones who never learned from their inadequacy.

"For all their shortcomings, trials had the huge advantage of placing promising players among the great and I have never under-estimated what they taught me in such things as aggressive persistence and the chance, if I was any good at all, to match myself against players who had been – and still were – my heroes.

"What was I doing there at Palmerston North, anyway? Three or four days before, I had been up to my shins in mud, socks around my ankles, playing for Wairarapa against Bush and looking as if I belonged there. And that spelled out clearly the one great plus of the trial system as it then was. It was the chance. I didn't have an ego to feed with my own tries. I took my buzz out of winning good lineout ball and watching the wing score a try as the result of it; or getting to the ball, flicking it up and watching a Tremain drive it over the line. My job-requirements were everything to me as a player and it was from achieving those that I took my fulfilment. Later, as an established All Black, I came to hate trials and their lack of player-to-player reliance. Team tactics and strategies? Nothing, except my own situation, had changed from Palmerston North, 1961. And I understood how frustrated the experienced test players, the Whinerays, Tremains, Meadses and Grahams must have felt years before.

"Playing in a team in which everyone knew the plan and that it depended for success on their own contribution to it . . . that was the heart of rugby. And trial day was also another day which brought the possibility of being knocked-off by some young bugger from the country – maybe some gangling kid with his socks around his ankles who had played for Wairarapa against Bush in the mud at Pahiatua three days before and looked as if he belonged there."

There were other players who approached trials with trepidation, knowing that within their loose, unstructured form there lurked the very real prospect of injury – and, worse, injury suffered in what, realistically, was a game of little account.

Lochore's belief was that if a player worried about being injured he would fall into the very tentative, fringing, head-up ways which made it a self-fulfilling premonition. They were the days, too, when injury was a bloody nuisance rather a personal tragedy. Where in more recent times, and even before professionalism, players limp off the field and into the physiotherapist's embrace, then, it seemed, players swore a little, gave their leg a bit of a rub and limped across the field to the next lineout or scrum and thence ran through the barrier. It encourages comparisons of preparation and of resilience under pain with the players of today. Lochore accepts the premise that the philosophical acceptance of pain has changed but also relates injury and attitudes to it to the social environment of the young and to the retreat from "natural" or "unconscious" preparation.

"The change in the lifestyle of the rugby player from the time I was a player has been dramatic, even revolutionary. To many players of my generation a gymnasium meant one thing: a barn of a building with sawdust on the floor where you could have a few scrums and lineouts when the weather was terrible. Going to the gym today is attending a scientific laboratory dedicated to muscle-building.

"Far from criticising modern ways I applaud them for much of what they achieve. The difference is that as kids we were endlessly active. It is astonishing to me that where in those old unsophisticated days we could do our warm-ups then go through some mighty strenuous training and rarely suffer muscle, ligament or joint problems, today they pull muscles left, right and centre. I am sure it is related to our youth when muscle extension occurred naturally every day. Our muscles had natural flexibility. We rarely sat around as kids. There was no television and the radio was usually on Parliament. There was always something to do. For us, if it was not a pretty daunting range of farm chores, it was making our own entertainment, building forts, kicking balls, chasing, lifting, stretching. Later, it was self-training in the rough, over the hills, down banks, into pot-holes but the body could handle it. Now, at the top level of rugby, unless a training surface is a sheet of grass training is off because someone might turn an ankle.

"I am a great admirer of the training techniques of the All Blacks, which force the players to reach deep into themselves for the ultimate effort they need to compete with and beat the set standards. Pinetree and I have watched Laurie Mains at work with the team and, almost as one voice, said 'That would have done us, mate' because training to exhaustion was our way, too, running the road in the early morning while on tour, making a race of the last half-mile, to maintain peak condition. It was our responsibility to present ourselves for matches fit to play out eighty minutes of rugby and to be pushing on through the last fifteen minutes while the opposition was flagging.

"There is concentration today on building chunkier, Mr Universe-type bodies. Muscles are shorter and bulkier, but there is less flexibility. The pain factor is interesting too. Today pain equals damage equals less than 100 per cent performance equals get off the paddock and get someone else on. We were strongly inclined to accept that something hurt, stay on the paddock and play through the pain at 95 per cent until it came right, which usually it seemed to do.

"When Danie Craven and the 1956 Springboks arrived here most New Zealanders thought a hamstring was something you used to tie the Christmas pork to the rafters. But by using faulty training methods on our heavy grounds, Danie and his unfortunate players pioneered hamstring injuries in New Zealand, introduced us to a body-part we hardly knew existed and, with that awakening, opened up for us a powerful new source of rugby injury of which we have taken full advantage. The only time I have ever felt a hamstring has been on tour when I was removed from work like crutching, fencing, shearing, digging – all those activities which naturally stretched the muscles. But now, to my deep regret, hamstrings are part of the language of rugby."

2
LEARNING CURVE

While 1961 with its North Island trial did not actually discover Lochore the great rugby player, it was a formidable year of self-discovery for Lochore the farmer. He was restless on the family farm at Opaki, constrained and unchallenged. Those years of practical farming had topped-off the agricultural course and his shearing-trail experience had brought him broader knowledge through studying the methods of other farmers. Now he needed his own space, a place to develop his own industry and his own ideas. He found it in Hastwell, no more than a decent gumboot-throw from the Eketahuna area where Murray Halberg first dabbled his toes in the dust. The 350 acres, 900 Romney ewes and 60 cattle were a barely economic one-man unit. One man is what he was. He was his own shearer, fencer, builder, ground-breaker, farrier, cook. In the hard times he had no self-recrimination. Harder times, harder work. His horse was his locomotion. In a measurable way, he was living out the fantasy of being the young pioneer farmer of the 1890s.

He had to borrow what he calls "a lot of money" to buy the property and the vendor left in what he calls "a considerable amount", to be paid back in five years. Five years later credit was harder to pry loose from grimly parsimonious finance sources and the farm was at risk. The insurance company to which he had faithfully paid his dues turned its back. He persevered and finally another insurer stepped into the breach. Another five years on, when he needed to expand, the original insurance company again rejected him. Being an All Black captain might impress a lot of people but it didn't wash in the cold, cold climate of farming finance. He was too small a fish for the insurance company and too big a fish for the government funding agency.

This was a crisis and Lochore reckoned a brief-case was called for – the when-in-doubt-display-a-brief-case method of negotiation which, when backed by 6ft 3in and 15st 7oz of passionately honest All Black farmer, would seem to present an irrefutable argument. He threw his papers into the black case, called on the insurers, made his plea to blank faces and, finding they were quite ready to let him drift along into the agricultural scrapheap, made some forthright judgements about institutions to which loyalty was a one-way street. He had documents showing that farmers who were not as efficient as he but who had bigger farms were getting assistance because of their very inefficiency. Did this not seem to be bloody unfair? The blank faces became blanker. Lochore threw up his hands, went back to the company which, amiably enough, had rescued him five years before and they, in collaboration with the Rural Bank, agreed it was, indeed, bloody unfair.

He was able to expand his 350 acres of rolling hill country to 500 and lease another 500 from Maori trustees. Now there are 4500 stock units and in Porangahau, Hawke's Bay, by dint of the years of sweat, some shrewd selectivity and a modicum of crystal-gazing another 1400 acres and 5500 of stock being farmed by the Lochore son, David, a farm-trained goal-kicker from way back.

Brian was always going to be a farmer even when he knew he was going to be a jockey. His mother knew it as she watched him playing with walnuts on the back of a card table. They were his sheep and he mustered them, sorted them, penned them and, in the enigmatic way children have with unlikely material, crutched them and sheared them.

The qualities of Lochore the farmer are much the same as those of Lochore the rugby player. His wife, Pam, a country girl and friend from childhood, knows much of the practicalities and the theories of farming and the crucial requirement for decisions to be taken at precisely the right time, whether seasonally or when the totally unexpected makes a mockery of seasons and plans. She says the thing she most admired about him when they were growing up together was his natural drive, the targets he set and then determined to achieve both in rugby and farming. He was prepared to give up "anything and everything" to make it work. "He instilled that sort of confidence in the three children and me as well. Where we might have had doubts about our capacity to cope when he went away on rugby tours he provided the direction and we just did it."

While keeping pace with advancing technology and new ideas, Lochore still relates to the practical wisdom of his grandfather Pop Wyeth. There is much of the Wyeth in the judgements he makes on the direction of farming and he will not be swayed by those who make other, perhaps more complacent, appraisals. The Hastwell property, windswept and challengingly wintered, is not easy to farm. Pam says Brian has always judged quickly what he knew to be right for him and got on with doing it while experimenting, too, with ideas picked up from similar dry-land farming conditions overseas. "I doubt that the thought 'can I do it?' ever entered his head." Colin Meads notes a striking parallel quality in Lochore's rugby and leadership. "Even when he took up the All Black captaincy as a younger, less-experienced man than some of his players, there was a quiet wisdom about him. He cut through bullshit to the reality and took it from there. There was no dithering, no doubt."

Farming became a full family involvement. It was the foundation upon which the children's characters became rounded. During Brian's absences on rugby tours they came to understand and accept that their contributions were as important as any to the farm's continuing viability. The realities of existence were before their eyes and theirs was an equal share in ensuring there were no break-downs in the process which safeguarded it. "Farming," says Pam, "never ceases to be a seven-days-a-week job. The family livelihood was there for the children to contribute to and they knew that if a job was not done there could be serious repercussions for the whole family. That's country life. If they could not go somewhere because the animals needed attention they understood. It was a very unselfish life and that is a great ethic for kids to learn to live by. They were never without the standards Brian set by example every day and when he was away through the heavy rugby years I brought them up to those standards."

One of the lasting impressions of Lochore as an All Black captain is of his apparently boundless patience, his unflappable control at times of high tension when others were dropping bundles and lifting tempers all over the place. Yet it was not always so on the farm. He could run on an extremely short fuse, not of explosive anger so much as of impatience and frustration if there were glitches in the detail of the day as he had planned it. It became not so much a family joke as a quirky sort of acceptance that whatever god-like status rugby and rugby people had bestowed on him, in earth-bound temperament he was human after all. Pam relates his rugby demeanour to his unremitting focus on what was required to achieve the result, his conviction that he was there to gather the players together to that end and not to be part of any activities which would diminish the prime purpose.

Rugby, she says, has brought the Lochores refreshing direction outside the relentless demands of farming. "Clearly, it was going to be a significant part of Brian's life and I believe, because I became involved in it with him, that it became fulfilling for us both. In the early days, being part of a country community brought natural acceptance that wives and girlfriends were part of the game. Then at the national level we were asked by the administrators of those days to understand that while we were welcome to the games the social activities were for boys only. At Athletic Park we had our separate little afternoon-tea room while the boys grogged-on in the males-only bowels of the grandstand.

"It could not go on like that. The time rugby takes out of family life is such that if the partner is not part of it there is a huge gap in what is supposed to be a total partnership. When Brian was first in the All Blacks I found I was able to relate especially to people like Ian and Don Clarke, both farmers, both having come through the country rugby scene. Brian said it was because they could never have achieved what they had were it not for having the same sort of support I had been able to give him. Now, rugby has become a total career existence and if partners do not have a full part in it relationships will not survive."

His second year of baching on the Hastwell farm brought, too, a winter of frustration rather than discontent in rugby for Lochore. Having tasted life among his heroes in 1961 he had a healthy appetite for more of it but was not called back to Palmerston North for the North Island trials in 1962. He captained Wairarapa from lock in all its nine matches, one of them a 43-0 beating by Australia, during which the Wairarapa players became embarrassingly familiar with the rapidly dwindling figure of Jim Boyce, the Australian wing, as he ran in six tries.

In Lochore's absence the trials were throwing up some interesting newcomers and none of them in the Lochore middle-row area more impressive than a young Canterbury lock named Allan Stewart. It may well have been that Stewart's emergence as a most talented lineout leaper, skilled ball-player and, at that early stage, an adequate enough scrummager was enough to put Lochore on hold as a player able to cover lock and loose forward. It was, however, symptomatic of the skittish and, at times, barter-driven nature of trial selection that for the New Zealand trial the selectors chose to play the Canterbury and Marlborough flanker-cum-lock Mel Dunne on the side of one scrum and a year later could find no place for him in 14 New Zealand trial teams.

Lochore, on the other hand, ignored in 1962, returned to the Athletic Park trials of May 1963, his stocks high following a magnificent game for Wairarapa against Wellington, newly married and having ever more to confess that he was the man who took his footy boots on his honeymoon. With the trials imminent and with the charming acquiescence of his new wife, his training gear was part of the luggage. He trialled in May to the stentorian acclaim of that one supporter who, following Lochore's elevation to All Black immortality, himself became immortalised in song and story. Approximately two million New Zealanders claim with their hands on their hearts to have been at Athletic Park when the "C'mon Lochore!" man riveted crowd attention in the early trial on to the tall, loose-framed farmer as yet again he matched himself against Red Conway. Sitting in the stand, Wilson Whineray found himself searching out this Lochore and finding "a tall, angular sort of fellow getting a lot of lineout possession and laying into a lot of covering tackles".

Even in the heat of the game Lochore heard every "C'mon!", winced and looked desperately for the sanctuary of the next ruck. "More hardened trial players might have been able to let it pass over them. But for me, just a cocky from over the hills in Hastwell, it was as if someone had thrown a floodlight on me. If that guy, with all that goodwill, had only known."

For all his embarrassment, Lochore was sorted out by critics as having played outstandingly well. *The Dominion* writer judged him to have shown the quality which would make him "one of New Zealand's most versatile and gifted forwards". Certainly he played well enough to encourage the selectors, Neil McPhail, Jack Finlay and Ron Bush, to place him on the side of the scrum for the final trial and from there into the reserves for the two tests against England. There, on the very edge of achieving the ultimate ambition, he trained in royal company. The loose forwards were Waka Nathan, John Graham and Kel Tremain, the locks Colin Meads and Allan Stewart, the front row Wilson Whineray, Dennis Young and Ian Clarke. He saw New Zealand beat England 21-11 in the first test and then watched Don Clarke kick a 65-yard goal from a mark to break a 6-6 deadlock in the second. Had he watched closely he would have seen Clarke, having placed the ball on his brother's hand, give a stunning portrayal of a man beginning his run-in while not actually running. It was one of those fringe applications of gamesmanship, exquisitely timed, finely acted, which inspire grudging admiration rather than condemnation. It encouraged the English to charge early and, thus, give Clarke the luxury of the ball replaced on the ground for a charge-free kick which, majestically, he converted to points.

It was a match, too, which presented further and compelling evidence to the International Rugby Board that the no-replacement law was applied lunacy. The England lock Mike Davis, having dislocated a shoulder early in the game, returned to the field to play on stoically with one good arm. His heroism was hailed but the message was ignored.

That Lochore's time was imminent became crystal clear when in the first of four trials to select the thirty players who would make a 36-match, four and a half month tour of the four Home countries, France and Canada, he locked a scrum with Colin Meads and then, in the third trial, with North Auckland's Eddie Dean. Meads remembers the event for Lochore's earnest commitment. "At that stage of his career you might have thought he would be feeling his way a little but he was very much a presence, climbing all over blokes to get at the ball in the air, eager and determined to be in the game for eighty minutes."

Having assessed him as a flanker, the selectors now knew Lochore could most adequately lock the scrum at this level – and then selected him to tour as a number eight, a position in which he had never played. It was, of course, an inspired selection for Lochore's attributes as a player fitted perfectly into the number eight qualifications. As a player in a provincial team which was often on the back foot, he had committed himself to tackling on the cover and to fullback support, he could jump like a stag at the back of the lineout and for all his lankiness and the suspicion of a knock-kneed gait was admirably co-ordinated, sharp of anticipation and quick to attend the point of break-down.

Those were the days when All Black touring teams were announced, usually after a nerve-wracking wait, in the dungeon-greyness of the euphemistically named social room at Athletic Park. A Wairarapa writer was diplomatic enough to call it "the refectory". Draught beer flowed. Saveloys dipped in tomato sauce and, with only rare success, wrapped in bread were deemed to be appropriate fodder for an elbow-to-elbow throng which, without premeditation, jostled the next joker's beer-hand with alarming results. For the players the beer and food were, anyway, an academic adornment. They made artificial small-talk which in no way disguised their apprehension. The ladies, as all women were known at Athletic Park, did their daintier sipping in another room, drifting out into the corridor when the announcement was imminent.

In 1963 Tom Morrison, as chairman of the New Zealand Rugby Union, told thirty players they would go on the 36-match tour. Among them was Brian Lochore, whose reception of the news was as studiedly sober as that of the old hands, Whineray, Meads, Graham, Tremain, the Clarkes . . . just as when they scored tries, players deemed it unduly exhibitionist to show any trace of self-congratulation. In the room, more emotional by far was Lochore's father, Jim, who was then chairman of the Wairarapa Rugby Union, while at home, it was reported, Earle Kirton's mother, smitten by the excitement of it all, irrevocably burned the family's evening meal.

Lochore played the first match of the tour against Oxford University. It was a match he found difficult, not because it was his first as a number eight, but because of its lack of pattern and the stop-start nature of it, forced by Oxford's deep sense of insecurity. It was, in fact, to be the model for many of the games on that tour with opposing backs flattened against the defence line while the British media bruised the New Zealanders with criticism for their lack of adventure.

When the team arrived in London, English journalists were

quick to ask the All Blacks to commit themselves to running rugby. Both the manager, Frank Kilby, a distinguished All Black of the late twenties and early thirties, and Wilson Whineray responded as one might expect, by pointing out that it took two teams to create that environment and expressing optimism – or was it merely hope? – that this would be the case. Whineray talked of "balanced rugby" and Kilby of creating situations for attack in depth by driving through with forward control first. As it eventuated, virtually throughout the tour the All Blacks were pushed by devoutly negative oppositions into creating second, third and even fourth-phase situations from which to free the ball to the threequarters. It led to the Whineray-charge around the back of lineouts, a tactic which engaged defenders and which gave its name to the world of rugby. The Willie-away is now an internationally prescribed move.

It was to be the aftermath of the third match of the tour, the first taste of Wales and the only taste of defeat in 36 matches, which took Lochore into a state of mind which was close to despair. But he says it brought him an understanding of the emotional difficulties for players – and especially young players – on tour and that this became the biggest influence of any on the sort of captain he became.

"We lost 3-0 to Newport on a rainy, dark day. Half-way through the first spell the Newport centre, John Uzzell, drop-kicked a goal and in another hour of rugby we could not reply. We could not even fall back on Don Clarke's boot because the Newport players did not once infringe in a kickable position. To say we played badly as a team is true but to say the Welsh pushed us into playing badly is truer. The Newport players were the absolute expression of Welsh rugby as it was then – mind-tough, body-tough, every player saturated with the history of the game and every player aggressively positive he was as good as any All Black.

"I know it is said that a team does not go on tour with a clean-sweep of wins as its top priority. I recall Frank Kilby saying the

1924 Invincibles held that title and always would and no team would ever take it from them, so invincibility was not to be an issue on this tour. Yet without actually cherishing the hope of an unbeaten record every young player on his first tour does think about it. And I would be surprised if every experienced player on tour does not do the same.

"That defeat weighed heavily on young players like Earle Kirton, Bill Davis, Ian MacRae and myself. I suspect it also weighed more heavily on the minds of the older players than they might admit. Certainly, team-selection in the weeks which followed was difficult for players like Earle and myself to absorb. I was getting one game every two weeks and that played hell with my self-confidence and encouraged the feeling that blame for the Newport loss had something to do with it. I was conscious that Earle was in much the same state and, probably, that he was feeling it more intensely than I. We called each other 'Wensdee' because Wednesday games seemed to stretch out before us till the end of time.

"When you're young and a long way from home and your hopes seem to be on someone else's backburner you tend to search for your own faults rather than to rationalise events with the realities of touring. I thought maybe I had upset someone in the team. I didn't feel confident about going to any of the senior players because, really, I wasn't that close to them. Essentially, I was still the young bloke from somewhere up there in the Wairarapa. I stewed on it, worried that people at home were judging me on the games I was getting. It was not the sort of thing I would put in letters home. I trained hard, went for runs outside team training, kept fit, but always with the nagging doubt whether fitness equated to more games. You convince yourself you're the only one this has ever happened to. It is deeply depressing.

"When I was at my most fragile I roomed next to Wilson Whineray at one hotel. I knew I had to talk to someone and one night I was in the act of knocking on his door when I stopped myself. I couldn't bring myself to look and sound like some sort of wimp, some whinger. You might say I chickened out but it was not a fear-dimension. If there was fear it was that I would be belittling myself in the eyes of the captain. Knowing him as I do now, of course, I know he would have welcomed the opportunity to talk me through it.

"Finally, over a jar or two one night, I talked to John Graham. He said it was a common tour complex. He had suffered from it in South Africa in 1960. He said I was doing nothing wrong, was playing well and the games would come. 'It's touring, boy,' he said, 'just touring. In South Africa I played only two of the first nine games and ended up playing two of the tests.'"

Kirton's reflections on the same set of events are less forgiving while also disarmingly self-critical of his own performance against Newport. "For a start I was without Laidlaw at halfback, which panicked me no end. I did not sleep for three nights before Newport. I couldn't believe I was actually going to be playing for the All Blacks. On that rotten, rotten day I was so bound-up with nerves that half the time I could not see the ball leaving Kevin Briscoe's hands. I would see him receiving it from the forwards and I'd start to run on to it then I couldn't see it to catch it. That's called panic. That's why I was able to convince myself I had lost the game for them.

"Nothing I experienced for the rest of the tour changed that. Before the tour I was just another euphoric kid so it didn't really register when my father told me I was going to be in for a hard tour. 'But don't moan,' he said. 'You're not going to get games because you're too much of a risk and those guys are not going to be interested in risk. They're going to be interested in winning. They have a good enough pack to win up front. Your sort of game may not be what they want.' That was exactly the way it was. I remember Frank Kilby coming to me after Newport and saying, 'I think you'll have to wait for your games now, Earle.'

"There were some wonderfully talented backs – players like Billy Davis, Spooky Smith, Ian MacRae, Chris Laidlaw. Their development on that tour was about zilch. It used to be said, 'Go on an All Black tour and learn.' But this was not a learning tour. All I learned was that I had to sort myself out. Bill Davis was distraught after Newport, inconsolable. I told him he had had nothing to work with, that I wasn't capable of kicking the ball across to him let alone passing it. BJ felt it but he tackled his frustration in a different way. He was a manic trainer anyway, but when he started to doubt whether he should be there he went the extra mile, went for extra runs. He'd graunch up to the front on team runs and foot it with the best of them. He had tremendous aerobic capacity and he had square jaws. Squarejaw Lochore. He wore the hair shirt and he ground it out.

"I, on the other hand? The naive young student, the scarfie, a bit vague, a bit airy-fairy. I was always going to be pretty brittle mentally on my first tour. BJ and I, the Wensdees, spent a lot of time together. We saw more cathedrals, castles and name-plates on old houses than the rest of the team together. When the tour was 22 matches old I finally took courage and went to Willie at our Edinburgh hotel. I stared down at the carpet – I could draw you the pattern now – and asked him what was wrong with my game. He said I needed to improve twenty per cent. Oh, I said, and went back to my room, hit my head against the wall and asked myself what the hell that meant. What did it mean in tactics, style, technique? What did it mean in rugby? It seemed to me the only people who might be interested in helping me were my old mentors in New Zealand and they were 12,000 miles away. Where BJ needed encouragement and reassurance, I needed a shrink."

Wilson Whineray is adamant that no player was put aside after the Newport loss. "No-one played well at Newport and we all knew it and probably we all blamed ourselves; more cause for the experienced players to blame themselves than the young ones. We had three specialist first five-eighths on the tour, Bruce Watt, Mac Herewini and Earle. If you take a tour of 36 matches and concede you are going to play your top players in the tests and in a few other selected games you come down to 26 or 27 games which gives a more realistic picture of the games available to the players.

"Brian's situation was much the same. We had loose forwards in strength On all those long tours of that time the biggest concern of individual players was that they were not getting enough games. When we left New Zealand in 1963 we would be looking at Kel Tremain, Waka Nathan and John Graham as being the test loose forwards – known and proven. But there were six designated loose forwards plus Stan Meads to give games. No-one was ever put to one side after Newport."

Colin Meads says that new players on a long tour tend to lose heart and, in some cases, slacken off when the frequency of games seems to be going against them. "BJ and Earle were not the first and certainly not the last to suffer. I remember rooming with Brian and telling him not to lose heart, to wait, but, above all, to be ready. The opportunity was going to come for him and he had to prepare for it. He did it the hard way and when the opportunity came he was ready."

Lochore came to acknowledge that after a comprehensively bad performance by the team the selectors were going to look seriously at shoring up the tour by bringing together the established players, considering the risk factor in players who had yet to be assessed at the top level. "They were shuffling the loose forwards around . . . Waka, DJ [Graham], Kel, Kevin Barry, Keith Nelson and myself. In fact, they pulled Stan Meads back to number eight for the Irish test, the first of the tour. I had no problems with that. Stan was a great player, probably the most under-rated player New Zealand has ever had. At that time he was in Pinetree's shadow but he became as great as his big brother; not as spectacular, not as naturally skilled but a truly immense rugby player, basing everything on commitment, determination and certainly the sacrifice of self for team."

For Lochore, what he felt as his limbo-time on that tour became the foundation on which he built his captaincy of New

Zealand. Out of all the frustration and angst came sharp understanding that individual trauma often lies beneath the calm surface of a tour. His concern for young players, their worries and fears, was the cornerstone of his touring captaincy. He did not wait for players to come to him; he knew how difficult that could be. But he sensed uneasiness and bewilderment and chose his time casually to offer his company to those players. "Within fifteen minutes, odds-on, they would be talking about their problems. These were players who, on the field, knew no fear. But it takes a different sort of courage to front-up to captain or management and ask the hard questions or lay out your problems. There is a built-in fear that taking that step could lead to a negative assessment of them as touring players. The need, then, is to be honest with them, but sensitive, too. The telling point is that you have invited their confidence. If I had success as a captain of New Zealand this should have been the most readily identifiable reason why – and it had absolutely nothing to do with leading players on the field."

Since his time as captain, sensitive treatment of young players has not always been a priority. Charitably, he puts that down to captains who as young players did not experience the need to worry about their own status in the team.

The tour left an indelible impression on Kirton, too. "In the plane on the way home I said to Bill Davis and BJ, 'Well, I'm going to make this bloody All Black side if it's the last thing I do because now I know how. I'm going back and I'm going to work my butt off. I know I'll be dropped and that I'll be out of it for two years – and that's because I've been a disaster. I'll get back, or I'll play so bloody well I'll embarrass them.' BJ said, 'It's going to be tough, Ernie. I don't know about me; at least I have the tests against England and Scotland to work on.' And Billy Davis said, 'Well, I'm going to have a real crack at it. I'm going to get back, you watch.'"

So, indirectly, Kirton says, everyone may have been done a favour. "By 1967 we were playing brilliantly. BJ was captain and

Aboard Winkle, a singular pony with a plural personality.

Crutching, a necessary evil.

Wairarapa Times-Age

Lochore with the prefects at Wairarapa College, 1966.

Captain of Wairarapa v John Thornett's Wallabies, 1962.

Farewell to a new All Black, Masterton-style.

Tyro All Black on a grey day in England, 1963.

Halftime huddle around Whineray – Tremain, Murdoch, Lochore, v South Africa, 1965.

Pinetree, a critical judge of my style, v South Africa, 1965.

First test as All Black captain, Dunedin, 1966. Mike Campbell-Lamerton leads out Lions attended by Alun Pask.

we had three marvellous seasons. The young backs of '63 became a fitting adjunct to one of the greatest packs, maybe the greatest, ever to play for New Zealand. Maybe, oddly, this was my success from 1963, my justification."

It could be argued with conviction that the opportunity for which Meads advised Lochore to be ready came not from his selection to play England at Twickenham on January 4, 1964, but on New Year's Eve, 1963, against Llanelly at Stradey Park. It was the 21st match of the tour and Lochore's seventh. For the third time in as many matches – Munster, Combined Services and now Llanelly – he lifted himself out of "Wensdeeism" and placed himself firmly in contention for more liberal selection. But when it came, a few days after Llanelly, which was a great game for him, the circumstances were controversial. Until the very death-knock it seemed to all the team, Lochore included, that Keith Nelson was the stand-by player pending a decision on Nathan's damaged jaw.

Lochore did not know he would be playing his first test match until ten o'clock the morning of the game. He had not trained with the team in London, as Nelson had, and he was mentally attuned to having a Saturday morning game of squash rather than fronting up to England and a capacity crowd at the spiritual home of rugby. The days leading up to the test had been virtual rest and recreation for the dirt-trackers. When it was known Nathan's jaw had, indeed, been broken in the process of scoring the last try against Llanelly, it was accepted Nelson would be the replacement. Lochore was rooming with Nelson. At 9am the morning of the test he set out for his game of squash . . .

"I got as far as the lift. Willie was passing and asked where I was going. I told him and he said, 'I think you should go back to your room. We might want you.' I went back and Keith was on the phone to his father. From his end of the conversation it was clear he believed he would be playing. When he finished the call he asked me what the hell I was doing back. I told him and a minute later the phone rang. I answered it and it was Frank Kilby.

He said, 'You'll be playing this afternoon.' I was stunned. I stammered something about having a bit of flu and he said, 'You'll rise above that' and hung up.

"If I was stunned, Keith was shattered and I could understand why. Back home his parents were assuming he would be playing; mine didn't know I would be and nor did Pam. Keith placed no blame on me but he was deeply hurt and bitter about the circumstances.

"I had not trained with the team all week, had not even seen them train for the test. I do not recall having a team meeting which related to what was expected of me. I had a crash-course in preparing for a test all right, but it was conducted by me in my head. I just tried to focus on the things I had learned a number eight needed to do, on defensive patterns and where I should be at any given time. There was no talk of my part in tactics or running lines. I was told I was there because they thought I could do the job they wanted."

Whineray says it was reasonable for Nelson to feel aggrieved and fair for him to think he was the standby player should Nathan be ruled out but that his participation in the test-team training was a matter of him being on the spot at the time. "As to Keith actually playing in the test, no such decision was taken. It was unfortunate he was not told there was no finality and that there were to be further discussions on Waka's replacement. The circumstances were harrowing for him as they were, too, for Brian. In the event, Brian did the job we wanted of him."

That job took Lochore through the diverse mill of tight-loose play as, through an inspiring resurgence of spirit, the England forwards fought back from a 14-0 deficit at half-time to clamp New Zealand to that scoreline throughout the second spell. My lasting memory of Lochore's performance is of trade-mark Lochoreism. In the first spell the New Zealand forwards took a fierce grip on the game. Down 9-0, England sought to embarrass Don Clarke and set up a points-scoring platform in New Zealand territory. The halfback, Simon Clarke, tossed up a finely tuned kick in behind the New Zealanders but falling short of the fullback. Simon Clarke himself led the chase but was so closely attended by forwards and threequarters that it seemed all would arrive at the ball before Don Clarke and in fine order to assault the New Zealand line. But it was a circumstance tailor-made for a Wairarapa player who had honed his skills on his provincial team's misfortunes. There was little Lochore did not know about defence under pressure. He flanked and crossed the English advance, arrived under the ball, claimed it securely and, with it, the mark from which he cleared the danger.

Kirton's recollection of Lochore's test was that "he ran all day, he corner-flagged, he covered, he drove. And the old heavies decided he was OK. It was the turning point of his tour yet I do believe Keith Nelson was the form player at that time."

His first experience of test rugby assembled for Lochore every segment of his education in number eight play. After only seven matches in the position he was still a student and he could not have had a more testing examination of his scholarship than Twickenham with its vast, booming stands, its lush turf, its strident demand for recognition of its history. The natural instinct for defence was his bonus but now he had confidence going forward and he thrived both on the freedom of the position and on the graft.

He was not new to Twickers, having played there against Combined Services on Boxing Day . . . "But this was different. The occasion and my own circumstances made it overwhelming. I was still coming to terms with my first test selection while they were playing the anthems. It was a strange mixture. Emotion, anticipation, some trepidation, pride, awe. It wasn't Wensdee. It was Twickenham on a Saturday with Whineray and Meads, Graham and Tremain, Don Clarke and Dennis Young. A dimension of rugby I had never experienced. But when the whistle went it was a game of rugby; and where I was, there were fourteen others who knew what they were about.

"No-one could leave Twickenham, having played his first test, without bearing the mark of it for life. It added immeasurably to my rugby character and the experience did not stop because the last whistle went. The experience that day, my first test, had no use-by date. It influenced my rugby to the day I played my last game."

He was to have his second test two weeks later on another of the world's great grounds, Murrayfield – but only after the tour selectors had thrown in an unscheduled teaser in the midweek North of Scotland match. Lochore watched from the grandstand as Whineray played number eight, an event motivated by the desire of the selectors to recognise the splendid form of the Canterbury prop Jules Le Lievre by placing him in the test against Scotland. "I understood and accepted the reason for it. Jules was a genuine test prop and would have played tests for any other country. But I looked at Willie and thought here was a new sort of challenge; here was a challenge I hadn't planned for. The skipper, no less, having a whack at my position and if it came off that was my second test gone. I have to say he was decidedly ring-rusty in the position and I took carefully concealed pleasure from the merciless barracking he got from two comedians named Meads and Tremain in the grandstand. For a struggling young number eight sitting there listening, it was not merely funny. It was meaningful."

There was another potential hiccup to a future for Lochore when Meads himself was placed in much the same situation in the third home test against the Wallabies the following year. Having locked the scrum with his brother, Stan, in the first two tests he was pulled out to number eight for the third with Allan Stewart locking and captain John Graham moving to the side. Oh, hell, thought Lochore, first Whineray now Meads. Australia beat the All Blacks and Whineray, reacting at the speed of light, sent a telegram to Meads: "And you reckoned I was a piss-poor number eight!" Lochore was more restrained, even out of Meads' earshot, but he did wonder where he might have been had Meads played a blinder. Where would that have left him when the Springboks came in 1965? "I might have become that kid who came over the hill for the trials in 1963. Remember? The one with his socks around his ankles. The one who brought over his own barracker. Didn't he get a test or two or something? That might have been me."

Thirty years on, Meads is self-mocking. "This wasn't 1960 was it? Me picking up a career as a loosie in 1964? Not bloody likely. Whineray just about got it right."

Having left a do-it-yourself farmer's life for more than four months of hotel living at such establishments as the rambling old Park Lane in London and the Caledonian in Edinburgh, waited upon at tables in umpteen hotels in Hong Kong, Rome, England, Ireland, Scotland, Wales, France, New York and Vancouver, having been wined where wine-making is ultimate culture, champagned at the Lido and ogled at the Casino de Paris, Lochore's return to Hastwell was an interesting study for Pam. These had been extraordinary experiences for a young rustic in the days before extended OE became every young person's goal. Pam found Brian needed occasional but pointed reminders that life was back to farmhouse-normal. "The habit of months such as those is not easily shed by a country boy. Coping with it taught me a great deal about positive communication."

Being an All Black number eight did not qualify Lochore for exclusive rights to the position in Wairarapa. Nor did he seek them. He played through the 1964 season at lock, thirteen matches on the trot, and although selected for the North Island at number eight was moved to lock when Colin Meads withdrew. This allowed Keith Nelson to come into the team at number eight.

It was Lochore's first experience of Fred Allen as a coach, but a comparatively fleeting one, barely enough for him to absorb the nature of the man whose approach to free-range rugby with breadth and pace, based on meticulous attention to the simple skills of the game, were to bind them securely as coach and captain two seasons on. "I was immediately conscious of the intensity of Fred's demand that discipline in controlling the ball, whether at foot or in hand, was basic to success in the sort of rugby he wanted us to play. He aroused sharp interest in players, which is not always the case in training, and he commanded respect. Having experienced Neil McPhail's more low-key, less expansive philosophy I found Fred something of a revelation – but exciting, because he placed all players firmly in the game. At that time, in 1964, the contact with him was just a taste of what would become such a compelling influence on my career."

Before that event Lochore was to have his first contact with South African rugby in a series which exuded most of the definable elements which make allegiance to rugby compulsive . . . the indomitable slog which made matchless drama as an All Black team successfully beat back a storm and a traditionally implacable foe (the first test); "The Occasion" on which for the first time in 44 years of history between New Zealand and South Africa the All Blacks became unbeatable in a series by winning the first two tests (the second test); the creation of fact out of a work of unbelievable fantasy when the Springboks turned a 16-5 half-time deficit into a 19-16 victory with a kick out of the mud two minutes before time (the third test); the final, gloatable nail, a five tries to none 20-3 victory and a series won by All Blacks over Springboks (the fourth test).

Wilson Whineray, having opted out of international rugby in 1964, returned as captain. Lochore believes the motivation was the chance to beat the Springboks in New Zealand after Whineray had led the 1960 team in a closely-run but lost series in South Africa. "Had it not been South Africa I don't believe Willie would have come back. That is the power of this rivalry we have had with the Springboks. In those days, at least, it took every tour, every series, every test beyond any other rugby experience. Nothing compared; not even Wales. This was my first experience of playing a team with that sort of historical mystique. No, 'mystique' is too subtle, too flimsy a word for it. The Springbok matches, compared with others, were a blood-rare rump steak as to a bowl of chicken broth. I had talked about it with Pinetree and Kel and I had read about it but to be in the middle of it was unlike anything else in my experience. Neil McPhail and Willie made that expectation very clear in our team talks.

"The public demands certain things of you as an All Black and it demands a lot more when you are playing South Africa. This demand is a tangible thing to the players and it places pressures on them spectators of the game could never understand. But underpinning it all is what you as a player demand of yourself both in the anticipation and in the reality of playing the Springboks.

"The 1965 Springboks were very popular with New Zealanders, so much so that after we had won the first two tests the public was saying stuff like, 'It would be good if they won a test.' On reflection I think corners of our minds absorbed that sort of environment and I doubt we were as hard-minded or as hard-nosed as we should have been when we lost the third test. We were confident, for sure – not to the point of complacency but sufficiently for it to just fuzz-up our focus a bit. When Tiny Naude kicked that goal near the end I watched it slither over and I heard this immense cheer from a New Zealand crowd – and a Canterbury crowd at that. It was like the roar I heard later at Ellis Park and Loftus Versfeld, but not for us. Never for us. Knowing we had lost the test at Christchurch and that the crowd was actually enjoying the moment, Ken Gray's brows furrowed and he said, 'Christ, this is the Springboks we're playing, isn't it?' as if it was inconceivable that, no matter the circumstances, a New Zealand crowd would hail a Springbok win over the All Blacks. There was a lot in it of admiration for maybe the most astonishing comeback in test rugby.

"I went into the first test still a bit of a greenhorn number eight, playing my first home test in a howling gale from the Athletic Park south. We squandered our wind advantage in the first spell to lead 6-0. Willie hammered it home that the game now belonged to the forwards and the halfback. We would take the Springboks on up the touchlines. It was raw, raw stuff yet it was that very old-fashioned quality that appealed to the crowd. They seemed to understand what we had to do, almost to become a part of what we were doing. Willie pulled us into a tight-knit unit and, with Chris Laidlaw controlling everything that came his way, we held the Springboks to three points.

"To hold on into the wind, to grind up the paddock, to be hoofed back again by a punt sailing with the wind, to take it in and grind, grind, grind back again . . . to be part of it, part of the physical grind of it and the containment of it was one of the most satisfying rugby experiences any player could have, more stimulating by far than an easybeat win by ten tries on a firm ground under the sun. It was a new experience for me. It added to my understanding that test rugby was as much in the heart and guts of its players as in the planning and tactics of its strategists. It was one of Whineray's greatest triumphs as a great captain. After it, the face of Neil McPhail, the old soldier, the old Kiwi, was reward enough."

Given today's standards of concern for the physical wellbeing of the players, Lochore would not have played in the third test. On the Tuesday before the test Wairarapa-Bush played the Springboks. Lochore is not an authoritative judge of the game's nuances even though he was, ostensibly, the combined team captain. When it was 3-0 to the Springboks he sought to stop head-on a mobile apartment block named Andrew Janson, who doubled as a Springbok flanker and tripled as a Springbok lock. The apartment block won and Lochore went into a deep sleep. "I played most of the game unconscious. I woke some time later when it was 30-0. I had no recall of events. I told flanker George Mahupuku he had to call the moves. He asked why and I said, 'I dunno, George. I can't remember.' So that was Tuesday with the test at Lancaster Park on the Saturday. But you don't give a damn, do you? You're never going to be a volunteer to stand down and give some other bastard a chance. That's called a positive philosophy and it seemed mighty sound to me at the time."

Were Lochore's position as an All Black in doubt before the series, match by match he advanced his status and cemented his place with a comprehensively fine performance in the last test. He can now judge the series less subjectively than when he was in the middle of it and he is surprised that in a test series between two major nations there should have been such a volume of errors by both teams. He had heard the cold appraisal of test rugby that it was not won and lost by tries and goals but by mistakes. Now he believed it.

His favourite story from the series is neither the debate which went on almost endlessly between Gert Brynard and Tiny Naude before the big lock took the kick which won the third test nor of any of his own exploits. It relates to the strength of the New Zealand prop Ken Gray. Socially, the All Blacks' favourite Springbok was the gregarious prop Sakkie van Zyl. He had propped against Gray in three tests and had not handled the long-backed, heavy-shouldered Wellington man at all well. In post-match debate with the New Zealanders, Sakkie, a most amiable man with a pint in his hand and another on the way, claimed he was the victim of the heavy ground conditions in the first three tests. "Give me a hard ground," he threatened, peering through a glass darkly, "and I'll show Ken what scrummaging is all about." Then he laughed almost with disbelief at his own prediction. "I will!" he said, "I will!"

This intelligence was carried with serious ulterior motive to Gray in the days leading up to the final test. "We wound him up and when it became obvious the Eden Park pitch would be hard and fast we screwed it up tighter. This would be the day of Sakkie's terrible vengeance. In the first scrum Ken leaned and worked his shoulders and Sakkie went down with that sort of audible wet squelch which indicates extreme distress. Then Ken lifted him and drove him down again. Sakkie exhaled loudly. In the end Ken got too low in the piledriver position, his feet slipped and Sakkie looked hopeful. But Ken's strength was such that he stood up from the collapse position and brought the whole scrum back up with him. Sakkie looked bemused." After the match van Zyl, in the company of All Blacks, was heard to comment wryly, "But I meant a really, really hard ground."

3

INTO ENLIGHTENMENT

The Springbok tour had been punctuated by much debate here and in South Africa about the scheduled New Zealand tour of South Africa in 1967. Here, the manager, Kobus Louw, and the president of the South African Rugby Board, Danie Craven, were overtly optimistic there would be an unqualified invitation to New Zealand; one which would ease deepening resentment that by unmistakable implication it would again exclude Maoris. However, Louw was in a position to know that the political tide at home was running swiftly against the prospect of an "open" invitation and by the end of the tour events in South Africa had soured Craven into acceptance that the tour was at least in jeopardy. In fact, by that tour's end highly placed forces in the South African Government had made such obdurate statements that the 1967 tour was, in all but the execution, a dead duck.

For the players that was in the future. In the present there was a tour here by the British Isles, the advent of a new All Black coach and of a new All Black captain. At an early stage of the trials it became clear the captaincy was a contest between Kel Tremain, captain of Hawke's Bay, and Brian Lochore, captain of Wairarapa. They opposed each other as captains in the main North Island trial with the other perceived candidates, Colin Meads, captain of King Country, and Ken Gray, captain of Wellington, both in Tremain's team. Two days later Lochore captained them all in the North-South match and three days further on was designated Allen's elect by captaining a New Zealand XV against The Rest of New Zealand. Were there another candidate it could only have been Chris Laidlaw, who had led the South Island, but he, too, was placed under Lochore's leadership in the New Zealand XV.

The interisland match and the final trial introduced Lochore to the many and varied talents of two Canterbury forwards named Wyllie and Hopkinson. "Grizz and Hoppy had put their heads together before the island match and had come up with the most brilliant of all possible strategies to upset the North Island: 'Let's get into the bastards.' Their close companion and friend Fergie McCormick might have had something to do with it, too. We trotted out there with our hair combed and our chests out, Masters of the Universe, and at the first ruck Grizz and Hoppy climbed in, boots, elbows, knees and all other projections flying – along with a fair bit of skin and hair. It sure brought us back to earth. Our chaps erupted, there was an almighty dust-up and things settled down.

"Grizz and Hoppy then put their heads together before the New Zealand XV match and came up with this brilliant alternative strategy: 'Let's get into the bastards again.' And at the first ruck so they did and with the same result. There were a few tag marks and crooked noses but it all added colour to the occasion and it gave Grizz and Hoppy the satisfaction of knowing they could stir up a storm without really trying."

Lochore's reported reaction to being told by Allen that he was to be captain of the New Zealand XV and, thereafter, of the All Blacks was, "Who? Me?" He does not recall it or dispute it. "Fred said something like, 'You're the captain and you call the tune. I'll support you whatever you do on the paddock.' It was difficult for me to accept that he wanted me over his senior players. Even after a full test series against the Springboks and having been very much a part of their camaraderie, I still rather deferred to men like Tremain, Meads and Gray.

"What was I? Captain of Wairarapa, whose ratio of losses to wins was one of rugby's most forgettable statistics. But they made it easy for me. Kel, Pinetree and Ken came to me individually and offered me their full support. I understand that in the dressing room in my absence before the first test against the Lions, Kel addressed the troops, saying I needed and deserved everything they could give me and demanding they give it."

Meads says that at that stage he did not want the captaincy of New Zealand, nor was he offered it, nor did he expect that he would be. He loved captaining King Country. He saw Whineray as "an elite person" who could handle with polish every situation on and off the field. "I could not envisage myself in that class. I really had no illusions about myself. I was more the rugged servant to the captain. I know that deep-down Kel wanted the captaincy and was hurt when he did not get it. But it was a measure of the man that he subjugated his disappointment and demanded support for BJ from all the team. We both had great admiration for BJ as a player, as a trainer and for his absolute honesty. He became, in his own way, as effective as Whineray, quietly commanding respect and admiration from all the players. He was a captain for every man. That does not often happen."

Whineray judges that Lochore has carried a great quality through his rugby life both as a young player and as a captain and in his activities since – absolute honesty of purpose. "He has never deviated from giving his top performance in all things. As a captain I appreciated the players who gave everything I knew they were capable of, and gave it for eighty minutes. He was one of those.

"The ultimate quality in captaincy is to have a team that wins games. If you, as captain, cannot deliver that you disappear – just as unsuccessful coaches disappear. There is no question that in captaining an All Black team you may be very able tactically, may talk with feeling for the game as an art form and with authority of it as a technology, but unless you have the quality to have the players go with you in the knowledge that you depend on them as they do on you and on each other, a team will fall apart. Nor does it stop there. The captain has to get on with the coach and, through the media, with the wider public. Brian had all that ability and that is especially interesting because he came from a small rural community, almost an enclosed environment, yet brought with him enormous natural instincts of fair play to the people around him and they responded to it."

When he retired, Whineray was approached by the New Zealand Rugby Union for advice on who should succeed him. "I told them, yes, that either Meads or Tremain would do the job well but that I thought I became a good captain through the learning experience while doing it. A captain needs time. My advice was that they should consider a younger player with the years ahead to learn and I thought Brian Lochore had a huge future."

Fred Allen was never in doubt. "We had Meads, Tremain, Gray, Laidlaw, MacRae, all with experience from the 1963-64 tour and Colin and Kel long before that. But it was my decision to make and it was the one least expected by the rest of the panel. I could not go past Lochore. It was that integrity. It was the quiet dignity of the man. Whineray had it. You learn quickly in the army to sort out the qualities of leadership in your men and Brian had what I always looked for – strength of character, the quality of quiet leadership to which other men respond. There is in it the capacity to provide discipline by example and demand it as of right while still commanding total respect. There was a resilience about Brian, the sort which creates the positive out of the negative. Brian would have been a leader of men in any field."

Allen wrote in his book, *Fred Allen on Rugby:* "The ideal number eight, the Lochore, the Spanghero, the Hennie Muller, the Basil Kenyon, the Duggie Elliot, is a tall, strong, versatile player who is capable of corner-flagging in Spanghero's indefatigable way, catching the ball in the lineout with the classic skill of Lochore, counter-attacking with the speed of Muller and pushing with the power and thrust of Elliot."

Charlie Saxton, who was to be Lochore's manager in 1967 and, like Allen, McPhail and Alan Blake, a Kiwi – the Kiwi captain and coach – pinpoints Lochore's natural ability to get on with all the players rather than a segment of them as a quality which underpinned his captaincy. "He would be a leader of men in any time and in any sphere. He was without ostentation; a big, patently honest man of the land who carried dignity and humility as part of his greatness as a rugby player and captain."

Pam Lochore says Brian took the captaincy on board as the next challenge and set about meeting it. "It was not something he had anticipated but if someone like Fred Allen thought he could do it he would just get on and do it. I know he was deeply affected by the immediate support of great players like Colin Meads, Kel Tremain and Ken Gray. When the captaincy came he was taken aback for a time. It occurred to me that he had always worked so hard to achieve the best that it was odd that when it happened in rugby he should be abashed by it, even briefly. As a man, the captaincy of the All Blacks did not change him at all and I think that was one of the qualities which they found appealing."

Earle Kirton, an academic observer in 1966, thought "from my position as a 1963-64 reject" that Meads would be appointed captain. "I thought if Pinetree was going to take over on the field when the going got tough, anyway, he might as well be captain." When the All Blacks arrived in Dunedin for the first test against the Lions he and Lochore met and Kirton said he was surprised the captaincy had gone that way. "I know now that Pinetree didn't want to be captain and that Fred didn't want him to be captain. Fred preferred to have him as a free agent. It was a smooth move to go beyond the old gang. Fred wanted someone who was everyone's captain, someone to whom young chaps would go with their problems – no hesitating at the door or kicking the carpet. BJ, really, had it all. Socially, where Willie was a polished orator with sincerity, BJ was sincere and very adequate, impressed everyone with his natural dignity and easy-going ways. As an on-field captain he was as great as Whineray and he loved the free-expression of Fred's sort of rugby."

The first lesson Lochore learned as captain had nothing to do with changing tactics on the field. It had to do with changing tactics in his team-talks. Like a lot of captains before him and since, he was given to the use of some vehement, though not extreme, language. He was a bloody and bugger man as opposed to an effing man. It was Charlie Saxton who said to him quietly that there was no call for that use of language, that it was degrading of him as captain and demeaning to the players. "I thought about that and I knew he was right. I never again swore in my team-talks. Some of what I have heard since then, both from captains and coaches, has been so far over the top that it has suffocated the message and that's crazy. It is also an insult to the players. If captains and coaches think explicit language of that sort is some sort of macho requirement to fire up their players they seriously underestimate what it is about rugby that inspires players to achieve their best performance."

His captaincy style rested on his unqualified determination to have the sort of rugby Fred Allen preached expressed on the field. It was much more than due deference to his coach. It was also an expression of his own heartfelt belief in rugby which broke the barriers of restraint and of relief that he was in a position to make it happen. Captaincy and its responsibility made him more dominant as a person and more expressive as a player. "In 1963 I was just a defensive player and a lineout jumper. In 1966-67 the confidence given me by captaincy and the style of play meant that I went out to attack as well. Under Fred we became a team with moves for every set play. At every set play we knew the point of contact. We concentrated our lineout moves outside the second five-eighth and our scrum moves in close. The art was to have every forward knowing where the contact point was and arriving there before the other fellows. It is such a simple philosophy and it encapsulates Charlie Saxton's truism that who gets there first with the most wins the day . . . position, possession and pace, the simple things done well. By 1967 it was an artform, *our* artform."

"I found I was thriving on the contact of attack as well as of defence. If Fred Allen ever needed a disciple for his belief that rugby was a game for fifteen players, for the initiation of attack from every available source, of taking up attack as the prime motivation, he certainly had one in me. From Neil McPhail of 1963-64-65 to Allen of 1966-67-68 there was a difference, basically, of mind-set. Allen created his era, stretching out of conservatism into open-mind rugby. Tactically, he was great but, above all, he wanted us to play a brand of rugby no other team in the world was playing at that time. It was much the same as we looked for at the 1987 World Cup and again in 1995.

"In a way our style on the 1963-64 tour was forced on us but it was, too, playing rugby to a style which traditionally had been a New Zealand strength. Habitually, from defensive positions, forwards won possession, waited for the backs to kick it into touch in a more advantageous position, then started again. Beyond halfway we started thinking about attack. In 1967 if we scavenged ball from anywhere and it was two on one or three on two we had the confidence and the licence to have a go. Suddenly, I saw so many more possibilities in the game of rugby than were ever presented in my early days. It opened up my mind. It was a rush of new understanding."

Conversely, as Lochore, Allen and the All Blacks steered their new course the Lions of 1966 were drifting, if not aimlessly then without a competent pilot at the helm. There was in-fighting, there were nationalistic divisions, there were all the signs of the inner turmoil which pulls players in different directions and which destroys focus on the truth that without close-knit mutual dependence in a touring team the only way is down. It started before the team left home, with the most destructive recriminations over the appointment as captain of Mike Campbell-Lamerton, of Scotland; such criticism that it was a fragmenting influence on his own morale and on his capacity to command with the respect of all players. During the tour, Terry O'Connor despatched to the *Daily Mail* a withering piece which said of Campbell-Lamerton: "As a man, highly regarded by all. As a soldier, refusing no challenge. As a second row forward, disappointing. As a Tour captain, stubborn in failure." It then invited all of Britain to bet against the Lions when Campbell-Lamerton was captain. For the distinguished army officer he was this was a deeply disheartening event which, by the end of the tour, had all but broken him. The Welsh were livid Alun Pask was not captain, the Irish were incredulous Ray McLoughlin was not.

Lochore says Mike Campbell-Lamerton deserved better. "Everyone was conscious there were difficulties in that Lions team. The clear impression was that the players of four countries were disinclined to put aside real or perceived grievance and give everything to make the tour work. If they did not have that intent they were going to be in deep trouble on the field. The term 'United Kingdom' does not cater for the deep differences between the countries which comprise it and when a rugby team of Irish, Welsh, Scots and English is cobbled together it has to have powerful management and captaincy. Sometimes it has worked, sometimes it has not. There are antagonisms of nationality which a sport cannot defuse. Scottish independence is alive and well. The Welsh do not like the English and the feeling is mutual. The Irish have complex reasons for their likes and dislikes. Composite teams of that sort also have to be winning. Winning overcomes all sorts of antagonisms and frailties. But with losses the Welsh point at the English, the English at the Welsh. That knot of Irishmen over there shake their heads, point at the English and complain they just can't talk to the bastards. The English look at the Irish and shake their heads in disbelief and the Scots wonder whether an all-Scottish team would not have done a lot better.

"The wondrous thing is that Lions teams, strongly managed, strongly coached and strongly captained have played some memorable rugby on tour. The 1971 team was the perfect illustration of that. With Dougie Smith as manager, Carwyn James coach and John Dawes captain the leadership team was

74

outstanding. It was as if the Home Countries had used 1966 as a guide to what not to do. The 1959 team was capable of the most beautiful rugby in the days when Lions travelled without a coach. That was a team of brilliant players – with youngsters like Malcolm Price, David Hewitt, Bev Risman, Ken Scotland, Tony O'Reilly – which played the players' game and made it work.

"There are those who judged that Mike Campbell-Lamerton was a bad choice because though his country was Scotland he was more English than the English and that he lacked the common touch. I would dispute that and say that any captain who is not given a fair crack of the whip by his team is stuffed before he starts. It could never be said that Mike did not try to surmount what became the insurmountable. It was not a tour New Zealand will remember with special affection, even though the All Blacks won all four tests, because match-in, match-out, the Lions were not able to play to a level commanding admiration. This was a particular pity for one like Mike Gibson who remained a great player no matter what inadequacies there were around him.

"The public view of those Lions was much aligned to its view of Campbell-Lamerton and that was that he was ineffectual. I could understand Fred Allen fretting over those tests on the grounds that the public judgements of the Lions would become, even if unconsciously, the All Blacks' judgement and that this had the potential for disaster. In the event, we won all four tests yet it is true that in the tests the Lions played their best rugby and that in the second at Wellington they produced a pack of such commitment that they set the base for what could well have been a victory but which became a 16-12 loss."

It was a tour, too, which took steep dives into volatility and steeper ones in two or three games to outright violence. Everyone, of course, blamed everyone else and there was a period of fear that the whole show would break up in a welter of charges, counter-charges, recriminations, acts of retribution, fractured cheekbones, broken jaws and bruised pride.

After the match against Canterbury, one week after the loss of the first test, the captain of the day, Jim Telfer, said he was not going to say the match had been dirty because every match he played in New Zealand had been dirty. The manager, Des O'Brien, said the Lions were heartily sick of the obstruction, short-arm tackling and other illegal tactics employed by teams they had met in New Zealand. "We went out today to counter tactics and this is the spirit we intend to preserve in the remaining games. We have had enough." The tour, he said, had been most enjoyable apart from the ninety minutes of each game – "I say ninety minutes advisedly; eighty minutes for playing and ten minutes for the inevitable injuries." O'Brien's concern lost impact through ill-advised exaggeration.

There was a swift response from Tom Morrison, as chairman of the New Zealand Rugby Union. It was not a statement to mollify the Lions and it followed a statement by Harry Blazey, the NZRFU president and a Canterbury man, that provocation by the Lions' persistent illegalities was at the root of much of the violent play. One week later, the match against Auckland turned into the bitterest expression of violence on the tour. Players from both teams were involved in punching and kicking and one Auckland forward displayed an imposing set of teeth marks on his arm at the end of it. A few matches later, at Gisborne, charges were firmly laid against the Irish hooker, Ken Kennedy, that he had so severely bitten the ear of the Poverty Bay-East Coast hooker that the wound required stitching.

As a first-year captain of New Zealand, Lochore was a concerned observer of the events which seemed to threaten the tour. He had in Fred Allen the staunchest ally in his distaste for rugby violence. "Rugby is not a violent game," Lochore says. "It is, however, a game which by its nature of prolonged physical contact provides the opportunity for violence. In my playing days players who kicked, stamped, butted or gouged were not in the game very long. They were sorted out by the players themselves because there was a natural rejection, an abhorrence, if you like, by most players of that sort of mindless act. Violence involving kicking, stamping and gouging should result in exile from the game. It is gutlessness of the most contemptible sort. Yet we have been slow to act meaningfully. We are so busy getting all outraged by a couple of jokers taking a bit of a swing at each other that the extreme acts of violence are inclined to get slotted away into the punch-up file.

"There are nice men off the field who turn into scungy mongrels on it. In my playing experience in New Zealand there was a player who so often committed dirty acts, so outraged other players, that he finished his career early, scared to go near a ruck because he knew retribution was waiting for him in the middle of it. There may always be odd punch-ups in rugby; they are not the real problem. I have been rucked out by experts – even by Englishmen – and it hurts when you get under the shower but that's acceptable. Any player who lingers at the bottom of a ruck deserves to be rucked out of it and, if he's honest, he knows it. When I became a selector I would never want in my team a player who was going to embarrass me with violent play. The odd exceptions slip through the system and there are players of the recent past and of the present who would never have made it through with, say, Fred Allen. Or with me. They'd have reformed or been tossed out."

It was too easy to take subjective sides in the violence debate. There was a further stirring when the Lions fullback, Don Rutherford, said he would never return to New Zealand to play rugby. It was, he said, organised skulduggery. But Ray McLoughlin, Irish prop and academic, told the *Daily Mail's* Terry O'Connor: "There were a number of incidents on this pious tour but every tour has a number of such incidents. In my opinion, only one game, that against Auckland, could be rated a dirty game. There were incidents in six or seven other games, but Lions' players were unfavourably involved in these. In the Auckland match, Lions contributed a fair share to the proceedings . . . I saw more dirty play in the Wales versus Ireland game at Dublin immediately prior to the 1966 tour than I saw in the entire tour of New Zealand. The typical New Zealander is far too positive in his attitude to be a professional 'skulduggerer'. The typical New Zealand approach is a delightfully straightforward one in which clearcut objectives and the logical steps to their achievement are not lost sight of in the welter of philosophy and theory which pervades rugby today. This is a refreshing change from the nauseating nonsense that is so often churned out on the Home Countries' rugby roundabout, the result not mattering and so on. All the criticism of dirty play in New Zealand has put a veil over the fact that at this moment in time the standard of rugby in our countries, in thought and concept, is well below the standard of rugby in New Zealand."

Lochore has good reason to remember what violence there was in 1966. "The evening before the second test in Wellington I was told I was required at Government House for a meeting with the Governor-General, Sir Bernard Fergusson. No-one seemed to know why, least of all myself. When I arrived at Government House, Mike Campbell-Lamerton was there. We looked at each other, inquiringly, shrugged our shoulders and were shown through to the Governor-General's study. He asked what we would drink. The night before a game I was not very interested but opted for a small beer. He said to his aide, 'I'll have the usual', which turned out to be a handsome measure of good Scotch. He said, 'I suppose you're wondering why you're here,' which was a serious understatement. He sipped his whisky, seemed to enjoy it and said, 'I believe it is important I should tell you two gentlemen that, in my capacity as Governor-General, if there is in tomorrow's match a situation of the sort we had in the matches with Canterbury and Auckland I will be obliged to get up and leave. You realise what that means, don't you?'

"It was a breathtaking warning delivered with geniality, but unmistakably firm. To me it meant New Zealand rugby would be shown up in embarrassment to the world and Mike was as conscious that it would be a serious blow to the prestige of

British rugby. Sir Bernard acknowledged it took two sides to create mayhem and his message was delivered accordingly.

"I have no problem with what he said. He was right to say it considering what had happened, especially at Auckland. He wasn't speaking as an individual but as a representative of the Queen and he believed that, holding this position, he had no option but to intervene. I went back to the hotel, discussed the meeting with Fred and Ron Burk, our manager. Then I told the players exactly what the Governor-General had said. Mike, who was not to play in the test, did the same with the Lions. The Governor-General did not have to get up and leave the match."

That was not to be the last meeting between Sir Bernard and Lochore. The day before the 1967 All Blacks left on their tour of Britain, Ireland and France they trained at Wellington College which is the nearest neighbour of Government House. Sir Bernard arrived in casual clothing just to wish the team a happy tour. After the last match of that tour, against the Barbarians, he told Lochore he would be sitting next to him at the dinner that night. "Over dinner he pulled a brown paper bag out of his pocket, just like someone about to take a surreptitious nip below table-level. It was a gift for me, an ashtray bearing a crest. He said in that clipped, military way of his, 'D'you know what that is?' I told him I thought it looked like a bee on a prickly thistle. 'Right,' he said. 'Exactly. Family crest, y'know. Bee sucking honey out of a Scotch thistle. Family motto: What's hard to do is worth doing. D'you follow?' I nodded and he said, 'Good lad' and pressed it into my hand."

The soaring climax of the match against the Barbarians – so breathtakingly and with brilliance won by the All Blacks in injury time – had placed the seal on a tour which brought such accolades to the All Blacks that it has become the benchmark against which all New Zealand tours are measured. The meeting of minds between Allen, Lochore and the manager, Saxton, brought with it such rugby that British and French writers and observers were transported into an almost competitive frenzy of praise. The players were excited by the open invitation to attack and were quick to absorb the requirement to base that on as close to error-free rugby as there could be. Discipline: that was first of the maxims. And the second. And the third.

Both Allen and Saxton still cherish the 1967 team for the awakening it brought in the United Kingdom that rugby, even with law-limitations which others found too daunting to challenge, could still be a game to excite the senses given the will and the skill to create freedom for movement.

Allen: "The British media were so sceptical when we said we would play open rugby. We expressed no reservations about close-marking or any other means through which opponents might seek to stifle that intent. We associated our intention to play open rugby with our intention to plant our roots in discipline. Then we went out and did it."

Saxton: "Just as the Kiwis revitalised rugby in the United Kingdom in 1945, so did Lochore's team in 1967, and by much the same method. It was the unremitting intent of the Kiwis to attack. It was our philosophy; it was an expression of my belief that rugby, without deserting its basic disciplines, should be fun to play and that within the fun there could be great success. As it was with the Kiwis, so it was with the team of 1967."

The unanswerable question is whether the team which so masterfully commanded Britain and France would have done the same to South Africa. The 1967 tour was an accident occasioned by the arrogance of South African social politics and a long-awaited stance against it by the New Zealand Rugby Union. It was organised to fill the gap created by South Africa's obduracy when the New Zealand Rugby Union advised the South African Rugby Board it would not accept an invitation which by implication or omission excluded Maoris from the touring team. Allen believes the 1967 team would have achieved in South Africa what it achieved in Britain and France. "This was the team to do it. I would love to have taken this team to South Africa in 1967. I talked with Louis Babrow, the Springbok of

1937, after he had watched us play England and France. He said, 'Thank God you didn't come to South Africa. There was no way we could have beaten you.'

Lochore has no reservations about the cancellation of the South African tour. It was time, he says, to make a stand. "The New Zealand public was right. There could be no justification for allowing the South Africans to dictate the terms for the selection of our teams. It was something New Zealand should have made a stand on long before 1967."

Allen was a powerful influence on what Lochore became as a coach. Although he did not model his coaching on Allen there were many Allen touches to what he did. "Fred's greatest strength as a coach was his ability to motivate individuals and from that to have a team function at maximum capacity, the players accepting that with inter-dependence came confidence and with confidence strength. Under Fred and Charlie I saw so many more possibilities in the game of rugby than were ever presented in my early days. Because Fred lived by the obvious truth of Charlie Saxton's belief that if you have the most players at the weakest area you win the battle, so did I. We pulled our heads out of set play and high-tailed it to the next point of possession. What we did when we got there was determined by the method of possession, whether the ball was secured and flicked up, whether we had to drive over the top. The backs were there to probe, to break the line. If they didn't break the line they put a dent in the defence and the forwards were there again to capitalise on it, deliver again for the backs to have another go. It was high-density presence at pace."

As the All Blacks of 1967 chose not to hug the line the game became fluid – or, perhaps, fluent – and that game flourished because the players had confidence in their fitness to pursue it. By nature, New Zealanders, says Lochore, are conservative. "It takes a lot of persuasion to get people to take risks. What made the teams of the late sixties better than the average is that they became convinced the result was worth the risk and the risk was minimised because support would be there in force when it was needed. We thought about our game plan and went out and made it work – which is a hell of a good ethic for players to lodge in their minds: This is the way we're going to play; we'll train like that and make it work. At the root of it, that was Fred's philosophy. While you're making it work the others are worried about defence rather than attack and they become easier to beat. The art of coaching is to persuade the players your way is the way to play the game and make them believe it was really their idea.

"Our pack was stuffed with provincial captains. We had utter confidence in each other. We were an arrogant team but only arrogant where a good team should be, on the field. We backed ourselves and we backed our mates. We backed Fred Allen and he backed us. For all that, the relationship between Fred and the players was not exactly Mills and Boon. Fred was not nicknamed Fred the Needle because he loved to sew. He could strip a player of any pretensions with a withering look and a word. Imperfections in training were food and drink to him. The fear of not doing things well developed into pride in doing them well. There were elements of fear of Fred's vengeance in how good we became as a team. He was ruthless but his heart beat for rugby and for his players.

"Before a team-talk he might tell me he was going to have a crack at me and that it would sound like a bloody good heave-ho, too. I could rest easy, he said, that it was to convince the team no-one was above a good bollocking. In the event, he would shaft me so convincingly I could hear the blood dripping. Kel Tremain loved to tell the story against himself of the captain's team-meeting the night before the first test against Australia in 1968. Fred was really worried about this test and whether the players were being sufficiently hard-nosed about it. I was at the front running the meeting and Fred was prowling ominously at the back. All the players were extra-conscious he was there and I was not going too well, either, with one eye on him. I invited the players to offer some tactical input. Tremain was in like a shot with the penetrating suggestion that we should give them a few up-and-unders early. Fred leaped, snarling, at the opening: 'Oh yeah! And who's going to chase them? You, you fat bastard?' Kel said the hair on the back of his neck went stiff, young players went a whiter shade of pale and Pinetree ducked his head instinctively. No player escaped. Pinetree once yawned and the Needle jabbed with heavy sarcasm, 'Am I boring you, Colin?' Piney took a deep breath, shook his head vigorously and said very sincerely, 'Gee no, Fred, no.' "

The response of some of the senior players to Allen's style was at first uneasy, suspicious. Some did not take comfortably to his lack of respect for their seniority, some were dubious, to say the least, of his run-run-run policy. Early, between Meads and Allen there was tension. When Allen told Meads he wanted him to graft in the forwards "where he belonged" rather than "jazzing around like a back" Meads regarded him with considerable disfavour. Then, a year later, in his talk to the North Island team, Allen needled just about everyone including the skipper, Wilson Whineray. Meads was not impressed. But by the time Meads' King Country-Wanganui team had beaten the 1966 Lions and Allen sharply and unfavourably compared Colin with his brother Stan, Meads was in on the act and there was a developing warmth between the two. At the end of the 1967 tour Meads urged all the players to take the Allen way back to their clubs and provinces.

Lochore says it was no accident that on the 1967 tour a number of All Blacks achieved the pinnacles of their careers. "Fergie McCormick, Earle Kirton, Bill Davis, Grahame Thorne, Ian MacRae, Chris Laidlaw, Ken Gray, Sam Strahan, Gerald Kember, Graham Williams – and certainly myself. Fergie responded magnificently to the faith shown in him by Fred and Charlie." Fred had selected him over the favoured candidate, Mick Williment. Mick was in the team too, until an eagle-eyed Ces Blazey counted the party and found it contained 31 players instead of 30. Before the team was announced Mick was eliminated and Ces, as a matter of meticulous habit, ever after counted the team numbers.

"Fergie always saw himself as a rough diamond, the kid from the wrong side of the tracks, and he played with that pugnacious edge. He was immensely strong but within the aggression there were wonderful skills. Fred judged that, beyond anything, Fergie would place his body on the line for the team. Fergie reacted so positively to that trust that at the end of the tour he was judged to be one of the outstanding two or three players of the tour.

"In his wildest fantasies Fergie would never have placed himself among the elite. For a start, 'elite' would not be a Fergie word. But I can say for him that on this tour he was inspirational to great players like Meads, Tremain, Gray, Dick, MacRae, Kirton . . . and he was inspirational to me as captain. I don't much care to sort out players for praise above others because, on this tour, most players gave what they had and some, encouraged by the coaching environment, gave more than ever they thought they had. But somehow I see Fergie as a special case, selected over a fine fullback in Williment and, for that, coming under some intense and critical scrutiny. He seemed to reserve his greatest rugby for the Welsh. His strength was, of course, quite prodigious and we knew he was indomitable in defence but if anything took us a little by surprise it was his speed and his natural rugby nous.

"Fergie and I were seriously into the communication business on the paddock, our roles being what they were. East Wales fielded on the wing a Commonwealth Games sprinter whose name, of course, had to be Jones – Keri Jones. I was covering when Jones got away on the outside break. I heard Fergie shouting, 'Go wide, BJ! Go wide!' I went wide and, quite deliberately, a little too wide and as Jones turned at full sprint to come inside me Fergie hit him with the most shattering tackle. Had Jones scored the game would have been East Wales'.

"That tackle created lasting uncertainty in Jones. In the next, and final, match of the tour, the Barbarians at Twickenham, he was in full sprint down the touch, but too uncertain himself to create uncertainty in Ferg. He had the break, he should have scored. Fergie was in a chasing situation which is bad news for your everyday fullback and he had to angle across toward touch. He had no right to catch the man but he not only caught him, he buried him in one of those jarring, bruising, horizontal tackles. Then the Barbarians had that brilliant Welsh threequarter Gerald Davies breaking, it seemed, beyond our recall. Fergie, from a standing start, took up the chase and as he descended, the wolf on the lamb, he was yelling, threatening the direst damage while calling the lamb's parentage into question. Gerald was harrassed into a rash decision to pass but it was a pass into our space and we recovered. As to Fergie's strength, I think of the Wales test. He went into it with his ribs heavily strapped but having refused pain-killing injections. The big Welsh wing, Stuart Watkins, was actually over our line when Fergie wrapped him up, lifted him and held him aloft, struggling to get to ground. He never did."

Lochore points to the Wellington loose forward, Williams, as one whose contribution to the success of the tour was never adequately recognised. Williams played his first test against England at Twickenham after Waka Nathan's jaw had been broken by a Budge Rogers punch in the Midland Counties game. "He made Ian Kirkpatrick on that tour. Kirky was always going to be a great player but he was better on that tour when Williams was playing because Graham was so good on the ground and Kirky was such a great runner. Williams was small as forwards go – Red Conway size – but his commitment never faltered irrespective of the punishment his body took."

On that tour, with only the 3-3 draw against East Wales punctuating the wins, Kirton thrived. Lochore, he says, was prepared to gamble, to take the risk because risk taken with discipline and skill was justified and brought profit. "It was Fred's way, it was BJ's way, it was Charlie Saxton's way. Charlie said we were going to play this sort of rugby, that we might concede tries but we would still play it. We would not revert to the stereotype that killed spectacle and dried-up the imagination of the players. We had the loosies to recover the ball quickly if we fouled-up so we attacked from set play, we attacked from defence and the blindside was money for old rope."

For all that, it would be a fiction to propose that the 1967 tour was all rugby at a sublime level. There were flat matches and Lochore has reservations about the team's strength in depth. He judges the 1970 touring party to South Africa to have been a stronger side over 30 players but that some of the players who comprised the 1967 test team hit their peak then and were on the down side by 1970.

The severest test of his captaincy in 1967 was not on the field. It came after events at Murrayfield on December 2 when the All Blacks' clean sweep of the tour's four tests was all but complete. It came upon an indignant whistle and then the command of the Irish referee Kevin Kelleher that Colin Meads should leave the field. Lochore knew nothing of it, buried at the bottom of the ruck from which Meads had emerged intent on laying into the ball before the Scottish fly-half, David Chisholm, got his hands to it. When Lochore arose he was conscious of great hostility among the New Zealand players. "They were appealing to me to do something about it, but I was unaware of what 'it' was. I was conscious as the ruck dispersed that a Scottish player was shouting at Kelleher. [Meads identifies that player as the Scottish hooker, Frank Laidlaw, and says he was shouting, "Did you see that, ref, the dirty bastard!"] The crowd was chanting 'off, off'.

"I saw the referee pointing to the stand and Pinetree walking away. I went to the referee and Pinetree came back. I had to ask Kelleher four times what had happened. Finally, he told me he had ordered Meads off for kicking a man. He said he had warned Meads earlier for dangerous play at a ruck, a warning I did not hear. He said he had no alternative now but to order him off. He would not reconsider. Nothing I said or did could change that. I had to settle the players down and get on with the game.

"So much has been written about the incident; so many judgements made, some in total ignorance, some inspired by patriotism and some more measured. Pinetree told me his earlier warning came when Fergie was getting severely slippered at the bottom of a ruck and he walked over it to get to him, even to take some of the leather himself. He said that, when he was ordered off, he was not only kicking at the ball, he actually made contact with it and shoved it into Chisholm's chest. Chisholm himself said to Meads in the dressing room, 'I'm very sorry. You were trying to kick the ball.' And Chisholm immediately came to me and said, 'He kicked the ball.' Film showed decisively that Meads was lunging at the ball and had made contact with it.

"One thing I knew with absolute certainty. I had never known him to kick a man and his attitude to kicking was that it was repugnant. We had talked of dirty play and our view of players who would kick a man were as one. We could not contemplate it.

"I was very conscious, however, of events after the incident and I need to say that elements of the renowned British justice system did seem to be strangely absent from the proceedings. No film was seen. Meads, within a corridor-shout of the hearing, was not called. Chisholm was not called. The hearing – which is a quaint word for it – was conducted by Cyril Gadney of England, Glyn Morgan of Wales and Charlie Saxton. Why Scotland was not represented is an abiding mystery. The referee's report was circulated to all International Rugby Board members.

"Charlie had let it be known that not only did he reject the incident as an ordering-off offence but that the ordering-off and its effect on the player were more than enough punishment. With only the referee's report on the table that committee suspended Meads for two weeks and added a rider which I thought reeked of crusty pomposity and insensitivity. It warned Meads as to his future conduct. Outvoted, Charlie was in the depths of despair. The inside story was abroad, too, that the majority of two which convicted Pinetree was under pressure to make an example of him, not necessarily that he deserved it but that it would throw out a warning to players throughout Britain that rough play would not be condoned. The nature of the hearing made it clear to me that the intention was to justify the referee's decision at any cost."

Lochore will tell you that in his view Kevin Kelleher was becoming rattled at that stage of the game and for that he takes some of the blame himself. Throughout the match he had been needled, nudged, pushed and generally vexed by the untoward attention of the Scottish captain, Pringle Fisher, at the back of the lineout. It was unbalancing his jump and affecting his delivery. Lochore warned Fisher there would be consequences if he persisted but Fisher, too canny by half, shrugged that off in the belief that Lochore would never become involved in a captain-to-captain stoush.

He was right. Lochore discussed the problem with Kel Tremain and Tremain, being the immensely helpful man he was, told Lochore not to worry about it. He would "fix" it. Lochore reflects that the joke in this was that Tremain was no more a fighter or a fixer than he. "Kel was just a marvellous, easy-going man who never had a fight in his life. Like me, he never got into scraps unless the provocation became extreme. It wasn't appropriate for me to swing at Fisher. So we organised the throw to the back of the lineout, I went up for it and Kel, with immense cunning, whacked Fisher in the belly. Easy-going he might have been, but he was a very powerful man and, given this circumstance, a formidable enforcer of basic human rights – like my own. Having done the deed he took off at high speed and when I looked around for him he was far away by the goal-posts conducting an earnest discussion with absolutely nobody about the beef market, in which he had some vested interest.

"Pringle was down in a heaving heap and, concerned skipper that I was, I hovered over him expressing my sympathy. I have to say I had less remorse than Kel because Fisher had been cheating, had been warned, laughed the warning off, got on with the business of more cheating and the referee was not stopping it.

"I could tell Kelleher was agitated at that time. He knew something had happened but not what nor why. As he stood with me beside Fisher I had the distinct impression he thought he was losing control. Through the years Kel and I were to discuss in more sombre moments whether we were really to blame for Kelleher going over the top with Pinetree. Between us, a punch became a 'Pringle Fisher' and Pinetree came to regard us with deep suspicion."

Lochore says, however, he came through it all without recrimination against Kelleher. That the referee had issued one warning and believed he saw another episode of dangerous play made his decision straightforward. Lochore's recriminations are reserved for the system which called no evidence when making a judgement which would mark a great rugby player for life.

Kirton watched events from what he describes as his own little grandstand, saw the sweeping swish of the kick from Meads and hoped he'd got to the ball before Chisholm. He is adamant that Kelleher's view of it was peripheral at best and that he reacted to the crowd and a couple of Scottish forwards.

Terry McLean, in his book *All Black Magic*, writes he was perfectly certain in his own mind that when Kelleher blew the whistle he was going to order Meads from the field. He says Kelleher admitted that the chant of the crowd was in the back of his mind, that he was conscious of the crowd reaction while he was making his way toward Meads. But, McLean adds, it would be grossly improper to impute that his judgement was swayed. McLean is, however, critical of the hearing process.

Lochore's concern for Meads was no more than his concern for Saxton who, angry and distressed at the sending-off, was all but broken by the verdict. "He felt, I'm sure, that he had let Pinetree down. Charlie's integrity was such that had he identified Meads' action as foul he would have had no truck with any defence of one of his own players. He would have been the first to stand up and say 'fair enough'. His attitude to behaviour on and off the field was that a first offence was a mistake, a second an inexcusable blunder.

"There was much to be done to pull the team together because that sort of event creates team trauma and with that comes the prospect of disintegration of everything that has been built up. We designated players to be with Pinetree, to share pints with him. My time with him was the following weekend when the match against East Wales at Cardiff was first cancelled and then, upon the offer of Charlie Saxton, rescheduled for the following Wednesday. Other than making unusual allowances for thirst, we carried on that day as if, indeed, it were match day. We lunched at the same time, had a few beers instead of a team-talk, had the after-match function and the official dinner. There followed the most heart-warming, hilarious night with hosts who would have given us the world.

"Pinetree and I crunched into the back seat of Jackie Matthews' Mini-Minor, proving someone's theory that great mass, provided it is very well oiled, can fit into a space designed for a third of its volume. We partied on at the home of Rex Willis, joined by Bleddyn Williams, Cliff Morgan and a very cross-eyed Fergie. There was a vague memory of pushing the Mini out of the snow in the dead dark, of being accosted by a passing motorist who asked for autographs and of agreeing, after earnest discussion, that we would need a good sweaty run in the morning which, by general consensus, would be Sunday. But things are not always what they seem. Some people lose watches, other ballpoints, others wallets. We went big. We lost a day. When Pinetree and I ran out into the wintry streets of Cardiff it was straight into Monday morning's crowds."

Lochore and other players of his generation and before have the greatest affection for the rugby people of Wales. He is saddened that New Zealand players of recent vintages have been unable to separate the parochial intensity of the Welsh crowd from the warmth, the humour and the abiding love of the game which is expressed in the clubs and by individuals once the fervour of the match has died down. "It is a tragedy Welsh rugby has been through such bad times, that they have been unable to pull their resources together administratively and in coaching. I know this, though: Wales will not become a rugby museum-piece. Its rugby people are too proud to live in the game's past. Their rugby blood is too rich for that.

"There are signs that the old zeal is returning. There was unmistakable evidence of it when they nearly upset Scotland and then beat France in that critical Five Nations match this year. That should be their building point. World rugby needs a strong Wales. We need a strong Wales. There was a time when it was as momentous for us to beat the Welsh as to beat the Springboks. The Welsh were never actually beaten; they fought for victory and they fought to avoid defeat."

The Welsh of 1967 were passionately competitive against the All Blacks but as a touring team two years later lost the tests 19-0 and 33-12 with a side which looked on paper to have the means to make life very difficult. Lochore says the Welsh do not tour well, become introverted and think a great deal of home. Those two heavy defeats, he says, were like deaths in the family.

To those players who resent the inexorable nationalism of the Welsh, Lochore says Welsh crowds are better at accepting defeat than New Zealanders. "The Welsh – just as the Scots, the English and the Irish – fill those colossal stadiums because it is a test match and notwithstanding a succession of defeats. They go *because* it is a test. New Zealanders display the same energy only when they think the All Blacks will win. Had New Zealand lost as many tests as Wales in the last ten years, how many people would be at our test grounds? Television is seen to be an acceptable alternative to actually being there. But there is no comparison, no substitute for being part of the atmosphere that makes a test match a rugby happening.

"And what of England? From being the most under-coached, England has become the most over-coached country in the world and with the transition there has been a loss of originality and even of the will to free up the game. They have always had great ball players but they tend to lock them out of the game, to carry them on to the field – the Guscotts, the Carlings – and then to minimise what they are capable of bringing to a game. Lock-out rugby. I'm glad in a way that I played briefly in the era of 'closed' rugby but I cheer for its abandonment in New Zealand. The rule changes have been made to encourage everything England once, many years ago, stood for in the game. It is a huge irony that, of all countries, that encouragement has been most obstinately ignored in England.

"Scotland has come a long way since 1964 and a significant part of that advance was due to Ian McGeechan's term as coach. He made no secret of his grand plan to have the Scots playing like New Zealanders and he succeeded very well. Back in those early and mid sixties the Scots had an almost primitive approach to the coaching of the game, more English than the English in administrative conservatism and this rather washed over the players, too. But they have taken coaching and used it much more cleverly than other Home Unions. In England you hear about the coach and not the players. In Scotland you hear about the players and not the coach. They are players who bond together well and, considering their small player-base, have done remarkably well for the game."

And the Irish? "The players who missed Ireland in 1967 and did not afterward go there missed one of the great treats of touring rugby. The Irish have heart and generosity of spirit and the rare power of expressing their warmth naturally. In their rugby the hope of victory burns as brightly as anywhere else but the expectation of victory is less compelling. If the expectation is not there, the actuality rarely is. The fans hope the team will do well. They do not demand it. They expect the players to be difficult to beat but not to win. It is that expectation the players absorb and, indeed, they can be most awfully bloody difficult to beat. In losing narrowly they rather lapse into the dreamy old philosophy that they did well, didn't they? It's all a bit like Wairarapa playing

Wellington. We lose 32-24 and think we've had a victory. We got so close to a major union. But hang on a minute, mate. If we'd played with the conviction we could win it might have been 32-32. I add this: Every rugby player should have the experience of playing against Munster. If he has not, he can never say with truth, 'I have been in hell today.'"

4

TRANQUILLITY AND TURMOIL

The 1967 tour ended, as it should have, on that ethereal high at Twickenham with the Barbarians first tied by a Steel-inspired MacRae try with three minutes remaining, then beaten by a Steel try deep into injury time. The last grand fling of the tour which brought Twickenham to its feet and which made strong men weep for the beauty of rugby came when Stewart Wilson, the Barbarians' fullback, desperate to clear his line, failed to find touch but succeeded in finding Lochore 45 yards out. No settlement for a draw here. Lochore ran, Kirton received his pass and found Steel, looming unmarked, shouting for the ball and receiving it. A sprinter and a goalline – high-speed magnetism.

The scoring of that try and the reception of it expressed just about everything which made of the All Blacks of 1967 a rugby fabric to weave legends with. It came after the defeats of England 23-11 and five tries to two, of Wales 13-6 and two tries to nil, of France 21-15 and four tries to one and of Scotland 14-3 and two tries to nil. (The Irish section of the tour was called off following an outbreak of foot-and-mouth disease in Wales and the west of England.) The one drawn match, against East Wales, had been saved by what might have been the most glorious individual try ever scored on any pitch as mud-treacherous as Cardiff Arms that day. Again it was Steel from ball flung wide, this time by Lochore and Kember, but here a Steel with defenders to beat which, impossibly, he did.

The tour also brought for Lochore a new and deep understanding of the meaning of perfect peace. He found it about four o'clock on the afternoon of Saturday, November 25, in the clinging, steamy, sweat-redolent climate of the All Black changing room at Colombes Stadium, Paris. The All Blacks had just beaten France in a game which for Lochore was the ultimate embodiment of everything he felt about rugby – and the most exacting test of the viability of the style of rugby to which the All Blacks were committed. It is the test he nominates as his supreme fulfilment in rugby.

"We were to play a team we knew was capable of taking us on in every area of the game. They had an immensely powerful scrum, based on a front row which ate other front rows for breakfast. They had Benoit Dauga and Alain Plantefol and Walter Spanghero in the lineout, Christian Carrere leading from the flank, and, as ever, brilliant running backs – Jean Gachassin, Jean Trillo, Andre Campaes, Claude Dourthe and at the back, Pierre Villepreux. To me, having played in the earlier match against the South-East Selection, the absence of Andre Herrero was, if not inexplicable, then a mighty daunting illustration of the strength of the French forwards.

"For the first time we were not so sure of ourselves, not so positive we could go out there and make our system work, not so sure that we could beat them back and forward. So we rethought our approach. I suppose it was another strength of the management and the team that we could do that together. Charlie Saxton came up with this wise, wise assessment of our position: create confusion. We started to get down to psyches. We reckoned the French became confused by the unexpected and when they became confused they were for a measurable time vulnerable because they did not know instinctively what the hell to do.

"Instinctive attackers from anywhere, the French, but inclined to fret, without instinct, when planned covers for any situation suddenly became obsolete. Charlie suggested we play a long lineout so we could work the blindside – that is, a lineout starting well back from the five-yard mark. We whisked Sid Going in for

Chris Laidlaw, another element of the uncertain for the French and Sid made a meal of it, quite brilliant. We played Ian Kirkpatrick in his first test, a player the French did not know. More uncertainty. He had a magnificent debut.

"As an aid to the implementation of our plan to confuse and destroy, Colombes was everything we could have asked for, a beautiful playing surface. When the wing threw the ball into the lineout our hooker was standing ten yards infield. The French were taken off balance. It was not that we made massive gains from it but it gave us a new initiative and had the French chattering. Should they come back with us? Should they hold their front mark? What devilish plot was this, anyway? Uncertainty reigned. Unsettled as they were by the tactic, they lost their competitiveness in the lineouts and when the wings threw long and with consistent accuracy, my job was easy.

"While the French were unsettled we got into them and scored our points by using the ball freely. We won the game early. Their try came late. They took a short penalty about their 25 and, frankly, we were too stuffed to get back to mount our defences to stop it. 'Go on, score. See if we care.' Little Gachassin's legs pumped at a rare pace and he zipped here and zapped there then tossed a super lob pass to Campaes for the try. Strangely for an All Black, I didn't resent it. The game was won.

"We played ourselves to exhaustion. The backs had run and run, had got up from some appalling midfield stiff-arms, and run again. The endless movement as well as the physical contest drained the forwards. The boys who had not played came yahooing down from the grandstand to celebrate another win and were met with a torrent of silence. Heads were between knees or flung back with closed eyes against the concrete walls; bodies draped on bodies. Nothing was said for twenty minutes. That is the most peaceful feeling you can ever have in your life – to prepare mentally and physically for a test, to take the preparation on to the field, to score the tries, to create the positions from which the tries are scored, to see a new plan unfold and bewilder the opposition, to win thousands of miles from home in front of a marvellously partisan crowd. And, at the end of it, to be hopelessly, gloriously exhausted. That is perfect peace. That is utter fulfilment. That is why we play rugby. That is why we become hooked on test rugby.

"It is worth recording, without being too cynical about it, that the referee for that match was Mr Burrell, of Scotland. He repeatedly warned the French for foul tactics, whether stiff-arms in midfield or skulduggery in the front row, while never taking the ultimate step and ordering someone off. We would not have wanted that, anyway. But he was also running touch in the later test against Scotland and publicly vowed he would give up refereeing if the decision to send Meads from the field was not upheld. In the light of Burrell's statement there is irony, too, in the fact that in the Scottish test Meads' head was still swathed in bandages protecting the wound he suffered when, as he lay on the ground in the open, he was coldly and brutally kicked in the head by the French lock Plantefol.

"He did not know for sure it was Plantefol until after the match. Piney, looking pretty rough, with a month's supply of emergency ward bandages on his head, went to Dauga at the reception. His French was as bad as mine. He pointed to his head, wagged a finger and said, 'Dauga. Dauga very dirty.' Dauga's eyes widened. He retreated, held up both hands and protested, 'Non, non. Not Dauga. Was Plantefol.' "

Lochore judges that through astonishing skill levels and the attacking instinct France is, potentially, the leading rugby nation in the world. He has never gone into a match with the French confident of winning. It is the nature not so much of the French game but of the French mind. "They churn out these wonderful players through a club system I don't understand. Their players have been kept happy through the years in the material things of life by a system I understand only marginally. Sometimes, with the flamboyant gesture I can't believe let alone understand, they drop half their team and come up with another which seems to lack nothing in comparison. They have a capacity greater than any other country to play an absolute stinker, where indiscipline rules. They have a greater capacity than any other country to play a game out of heaven – so comprehensively admirable that it is cheered by the supporters of the country they have beaten. They have a greater capacity than any other country to reverse an apparent loss and make it a stunning victory with just one magical movement from inside their own 22. They are the cheeky little streetkids of international rugby but they are also the sophisticates. How much poorer rugby would have been without players like Maso, Gachassin, Blanco, Boniface, Villepreux, Herrero, Carrere, Spanghero, Cester and so many others. If only they had the discipline to match the flair – or is that asking for the moon?

"When the French came to New Zealand in 1968 we were in much the same mode mentally as in 1967. As usual we were under strict instructions to get on with the game and reject the temptation to become involved in the sort of retaliatory skirmishes which seem to infect matches with France. I was still in recovery from an injury suffered in the first of two tests on the earlier Australian tour and missed the first test against France. The second was the dirtiest match I have ever been involved in. I saw Laidlaw kicked in the head, Bruce McLeod kicked in the head, Meads kneed in the face. I must say also that I saw actions from upset All Blacks which were regrettable.

"Scrums and rucks were made to order for the game's thugs and their skipper Marcel Puget was being a right little ratbag, stupidly abrasive, yapping like a terrier, stirring up trouble. My players were coming to me and telling me they could not go on just absorbing it. I had to do something. I placated them as long as possible then I had had enough. In an animated little scene, unflatteringly captured on camera, I told the referee, John Pring, I had had enough. If he didn't stop the violence I would let my players go. That was not a good thing to say to a referee and John did not take it kindly. But it was that or, undoubtedly, the game would have blown sky-high. After it there were allegations of violence from both sides, there were calls for neutral referees, there were rejections of neutral referees, there was the awful odour of the same acrimony which had soured the 1966 Lions tour. For all that, it was the test no-one remembers for anything much at all other than Villepreux's staggering goal from a distance variously estimated as being from 65 yards to one mile.

"John Pring had a long memory. Three years later, in circumstances which will become clear, I agreed to come out of recent retirement to play the third test against the 1971 Lions at Athletic Park. Pinetree was the All Black captain but I must admit a few times I rather forgot myself and passed a terse word or two of complaint to the referee who, by chance, was Pring. After one comparatively mild expression of my concern John followed me across the field to a lineout where he accosted me and asked, rather bitingly, I thought, 'Are you the captain of this team?' There was no smart answer and I subsided without a whimper. I guess that made it 1-1."

The All Blacks completed a 3-0 series win over the French at Auckland in the sort of match the game's devoted followers were desperate to see, a match in New Zealand to equal the brilliance, the drama and the humour of the 1967 match in Paris and to cast to hell the awful spectacle of Wellington. For Lochore it was both triumph and relief. "No-one, and least of all myself, takes pleasure in a game which is ill-tempered from beginning to end. It sours a victory and it makes a loss even more depressing. There was a requirement on both teams to lift themselves above all the hostility generated at Athletic Park. Only by achieving that first could we possibly demonstrate the sort of rugby we had played in 1967. There had been obstacles to it in Australia and that had left the team feeling a bit flattened. In that sense, Auckland revived our own pride in ourselves."

The Australian tour was a fateful one for New Zealand rugby. Out of one episode in it there emerged for Fred Allen such deepening disillusionment with the New Zealand Rugby Union that he made his decision to see the team through the tour by France and then to retire. Allen's relationships with some at the top of the national administration had not run smoothly. He tired of what he judged to be pin-pricking pedantry and he felt hounded by action and word which betrayed a stick-in-the-mud conservatism rather than a liberal understanding and endorsement of where he was taking All Black rugby. He found himself to be under scrutiny in which there was identifiable malice. Given all the evidence, a neutral judge in these matters would most likely have found in his favour.

During this tour and before it, Allen was open-handed in his co-operation with other coaches, willing to spread the word and to give advice. He laughed at the growing custom of holding "secret" training sessions and invited all reporters, observers, players and spies to attend All Black training. It was in this light that, before the first test in Sydney, as a touring correspondent, I approached Fred and asked if I could attend his team-talk and from it write a backgrounder. Fred did not hesitate. Be there at this time, he said. In the event I was conscious of some disapproving stares from senior All Blacks. I openly took notes of what was for me a most enlightening study of motivation in action.

I wrote my story. It appeared the following morning in *The Dominion*. By 7am, Australian time, the team manager, Duncan Ross, was roused from a deep sleep by the chairman of the New Zealand Rugby Union, Tom Morrison, who was in a state of high indignation – as, it seems, were other senior administrators. The gist of a longish call was that my presence at the team-talk contravened traditional practice and that my story had no place in the public domain. It was, in short, disgraceful and Mr Allen should be apprised of the union's deepest displeasure. Ross passed the message along with feeling, Allen was furious, having understood I had attended the meeting for background (as opposed to writing a backgrounder), and I was up the legendary creek, but with one paddle. Having told Fred I had never disguised my intention to write a story, I showed him the copy. He read it, gave it a qualified pass mark and over a drink opened up his heart. I had no doubt at that time that by season's end he would tell the union enough was enough.

The All Blacks, looking beyond Wales in 1969 and into South Africa, 1970, were, to put it mildly, disappointed. Lochore had the highest hopes of the team staying together and recovering, with Allen, the touring glories of 1967. Allen has made it clear he was burning to take the team to South Africa in 1967 and, when that tour was abandoned, he says, his anticipation of a tour there in 1970 was just as sharp. That being so, the measure of his disaffection with the New Zealand Rugby Union may be better judged.

Lochore admits he was not unconscious of problems Allen was having with the union but was ignorant of how tense that relationship had become. "Fred was also frustrated by the nature of the two tests in Australia. I think he felt let-down that an old student of his with Auckland, Des Connor, then coaching Australia, set up such suffocating defensive systems that the game in Australia was done a serious disservice. At the heart of it was disappointment that we were not able to display the sort of rugby we wanted to – needed to, in a way. Connor, I think, did what he felt he had to do with a young team and if that meant putting the shutters up at the first whistle, so be it.

"My part in it ended, anyway, about half-way through the first spell. My left thumb had parted company with much of my hand about ten minutes into the game and I finally conceded when the disability was compounded by a hamstring strain fifteen minutes later. Some might say it was an act of God. Ian Kirkpatrick came on and transformed the game, scoring three tries in a great performance. The second test was the one of the infamous, to Australians, and justifiable, to New Zealanders, award of a penalty try which gave us a 19-18 win at the last gasp. I can only say that, as a distant and subjective observer, and after searching my conscience, I could find, just marginally, cause for the award of the try."

Since the sixties, no country has so advanced in Lochore's esteem as Australia. He says that in 1968 they were still a country which, almost by chance it seemed, threw into the arena individuals of quite startling ability, from time to time gathered together formidable teams, but always played with a colossal will to win, and never more so than when they played New Zealand. "In attitude they are very much like us. The game suits them. They do not have a vast player-base yet produce fine, well-drilled teams. Imagine all those rugby league players playing union. What a team they would have then. Australia's advance has done rugby immeasurable good here. They are just a couple of hours away and are everything we could want as an opponent. Their place in the competitive esteem of New Zealanders has gone beyond any other of our traditional opponents except South Africa and I would place them on equal terms."

For everything he felt in loss of both a mentor and a kindred spirit when Allen irrevocably cried enough, Lochore stands to the defence of his successor, Ivan Vodanovich, an All Black prop in 1955, who may well have suffered most when, after the All Blacks lost the series against South Africa in 1970, the public made its judgements. It was not understood, Lochore says, that Vodanovich was a thorough thinker on the game and, though his training methods were basic, he sent teams on to the field well motivated and with much the same brief to play expressive rugby as they had from Allen. "I know it became the great tour defence – that is, in its rugby terms – that in winning all the provincial games we made it a success. I was decidedly uncomfortable with that judgement when it was delivered by the manager, Ron Burk, and on reflection I cannot live with it now. We failed in what was the most fiercely burning ambition of my time: to beat South Africa in a series in South Africa. Were I to believe the tour was a success how could I explain the deep depression I felt at the end of it?"

Before South Africa, New Zealand hosted a Welsh team with outstanding players but with little coherence – "Lacking common purpose," Lochore says. They were offered and accepted a difficult little tour with two tests in five games and were able to beat Wellington and Otago. Individuals played some teasingly deft rugby but, confronted by an All Black team playing with much the same ardour and intent to spread the game as in 1967, the Welsh were comprehensively outplayed in both tests. Vodanovich had taken over as coach but there was no discernible switch of emphasis. "Publicly, Ivan distanced himself from the Allen era. He was his own man and his own coach but he was well advised to take what was already there, ensure its fitness and turn it loose on the Welsh. What came of this was rugby from which the players took renewed confidence."

The 1970 tour went ahead in the face of such threat of dire events that the All Blacks were driven in the early morning hours by back roads and byways to their aircraft on the tarmac at Wellington Airport. Although the South Africans had succumbed to the demand, if not for an open invitation then one which could be interpreted as such, protest lingered and gathered momentum until the Federation of Labour uneasily shifted ground and edged out of the protest arena. A restraining order was sought under an ancient law, naming Burk, Vodanovich, Lochore and Kember. It was duly considered by a Supreme Court judge and declined. A New Zealand team containing three players of Maori blood, Buff Milner, Blair Furlong and Sid Going, and one of Polynesian blood, Bryan Williams, left New Zealand to tour South Africa.

The surreptitious manner of leaving angered and depressed Lochore. He says it was as if people were accusing him of being a supporter of apartheid whereas he found apartheid indefensible. "Judgement of the players in that way, on the grounds that they were supporting one of the bastions of apartheid, white rugby, took no account of what were exceptional circumstances that year. As I have said, the New Zealand Rugby Union should have taken its stance on the invitation long, long before 1967. By not doing that it meant we had succumbed to their regime – had, in effect, given South Africa a voice in the

Charging to the line, Lions 1966.

Fred Allen, needle sheathed, talks tactics, 1967.

Fergie meets the Queen, Twickenham, 1967.

The greatest test . . . v France, 1967. Demonstrating half-back technique to Sid Going. Less academic from Spanghero, Dauga, Plantefol and Abadie.
Overleaf: The three of us, v England, 1967. (John Blackwell collection)

Above and Opposite: Two faces of rugby. Confrontation (during) and civilisation (after) second test, 1968 – with French captain Marcel Puget (and referee John Pring).

Brian Lochore

110

Brian Lochore

NZ Newspapers

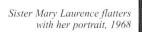

*Sister Mary Laurence flatters
with her portrait, 1968*

Half-time reappraisal, 1968.

Pre-test prayer meeting. Athletic Park

selection of the All Blacks. That rankles with me to this day.

"We felt very strongly as players that we were breaking new ground, creating history positively, making a dent in apartheid. There was pride in that because it could have been the beginning of something much, much bigger. I felt in my heart of hearts that I was doing something to help everyone in South Africa – the black people by encouraging them that there were equal societies where black and white could live together and play together. We communicated with many black people on level terms and I know from their response that in our small way we were able to make them feel they were not alone in their struggle. We didn't change a nation, but we stimulated and encouraged.

"If there were those who had not thought sufficiently what apartheid meant they received a sharp education after the match at Kimberley against Griqualand West when black supporters raced to get near their idol, Bryan Williams. The spectacle which followed, as whites moved in with fists and boots, was sickening, degrading. After the tour I spoke many times of the country as we found it. Nothing I said in defence of the tour could satisfy those whose minds had hardened against it. I would still say that even if it were only because we broke the ice, the tour was worth while."

Lochore captained New Zealand in 18 tests. Only three were lost, and all on that tour of South Africa. That lingers, still triggers self-debate. He wishes the team had played its best rugby when it mattered. He wishes that in planning for the tour respect for the South Africans had been higher. He regrets there were 10 matches before the first test – an inordinately long time for the South Africans to analyse the All Blacks' style and their own options to overcome it . . . "And I doubt that, as the tour developed, we settled on the right game plan. We always felt that to beat the South Africans we needed to move the ball, to run their big forwards around. Probably that was a fair call, but two things happened in the tests which destroyed it. First, we made simple errors which negated our ability to see the plan through.

Second, where in the provincial games the advantage law was applied almost without exception, when it came to the tests it was ignored. It was an inconsistency which played directly into the Springboks' hands because they were very happy to move from scrum to lineout to scrum and so on.

"We, of course, compounded the problem by error. But application of the advantage law in the tests would have given us our springboard. Though we were reminded by a lot of people that what we had beaten in the provinces was as nothing compared with Springboks when they put on green and gold we were rather conned – or had conned ourselves – by the sweep through the provincial teams. As individuals playing for their provinces, Springboks hadn't bothered us much at all. We saw ourselves as having the mobility to run them out of the tests. The first test demolished that confidence."

Harsh words about the objectivity of the test referees flowed but Lochore will not take that refuge. He says the Springboks were better prepared to play test rugby than were the All Blacks. He is, however, unbelieving that it took so long for the introduction to test rugby of neutral referees. "There is a strong tendency for New Zealanders to look back at South Africa and what they have judged to be refereeing inconsistencies at best and unabashed patriotism at worst. South Africans, British and French used to come here and lay the same complaints. The French of 1968 were bitterly critical of our referees. I would say neutral referees would have been an assistance in 1970 but I doubt whether that would have been sufficient for us to win the series. We have to look elsewhere and, principally, at ourselves. I felt throughout my international career that neutral referees were essential.

"There were so many hard feelings about the refereeing that it seemed clear to me that the neutral option was desirable for the game and for the relationships between players and countries. From the outset of my All Black captaincy I pleaded the cause of neutral referees with the New Zealand Rugby Union and with anyone else who would listen. I was knocked over by the resentment I met. Red rag to a bull. The logic of it meant nothing. Administrators fell back on the amateur ethic and the spirit of the game as a defence for the status quo while the spirit of the game was being knocked to smithereens by the antagonisms which built up over refereeing. Nothing upset the players more than inconsistent interpretation of the laws from country to country. We could, and should, have had neutral referees travelling the world ten years before the traditionalists finally retreated or retired. Uniformity would logically have followed. I have heard that the South African Rugby Board offered the New Zealand Rugby Union neutral referees for 1976 and that this was rejected on the grounds that it would be an insidious intrusion on the spirit of the game. Yet the rancour caused by the test refereeing in 1976 persists to this day."

Kirton's recall of events in the second and third tests in 1970 is of refereeing and touch-judging which was, at best, selective. "I must admit that some of the fine players of 1967 were not as fine in 1970. Players would say with a little justification, for instance, that I was past my best. I was not alone in that. The same might be said of Billy Davis, Ian MacRae, Malcolm Dick. We were fit but within our fitness lacked sharpness. I think what troubled some of the team was that at crucial times experience was discarded. We threw a scare into South Africans by the manner in which we creamed their top provincial sides. It had never happened to them before. They went out to find twelve men who were just going to smack us over. And they found them. And their ability to smack us over was complemented by the licence they were given to do it. In our minds, we expected to go out in the first test and win it cruising. That was never going to happen. Simply, they king-hit us, thrashed us.

"In the second test Bill Davis undoubtedly scored from a chip-kick by me. Scored? He did but he didn't. Clearly in my view, he dived on the ball for the try. The referee, Wynand Malan, said he had knocked-on in goal. There was no knock-on.

Bryan Williams clearly scored in a corner, the referee signalled the try, the touch-judge, Max Baise, signalled no try. The defender who tackled Williams touched the corner-flag; Williams did not. Laidlaw went to Baise and said, 'Max, you're not competent to be on the touchline if you rule like that.' Cheating? No. Let's say it was just incompetence. Max refereed the third test. Joggie Jansen and Mannie Roux shattered our midfield while stealing space under Max's nose. I was knocked silly twice by the loosie Jan Ellis, hit before I had the ball. These offences were confined to our half, out of Fergie's kicking range. Chris again went to Baise, pointed at Ellis, and said, 'You know what he's doing, Max. Why don't you send him off for persistent infringement?' Max said he couldn't do that in an international. Chris said, 'Well, you shouldn't bloody well be here.'"

Lochore sat out the first five matches of the tour, recovering from a hand injury suffered in one of the two whistle-stop matches at Perth. From town to town he sought a co-operative doctor who might remove the plaster and proclaim him fit. He returned for the sixth match, against Eastern Transvaal. Meads had assumed the captaincy and his performance in the first four matches was the finest of his career. He was sensational, so sensational that a young man like Bryan Williams believed the All Blacks with Meads to be invincible.

Then came Eastern Transvaal at Springs, Lochore's first game and Meads' last until after the second test, nine matches on. In a brawling, booting, pig of a match he was kicked on the arm and it was broken. Lochore to this day is in awe of the form Meads had been in. "He was something to behold. I had measured him as great in many games but here he was just stupendous. His was rugby of the sort to bring surging confidence to the rest of the team. He would have been a dominating figure in the tests. As much as he did damned well when he came back he was not the same player, well removed from the same force. I cannot say with conviction that he was deliberately kicked, but certainly he was kicked as he lay on the ground."

With some degree of unease, Kirton claims to have been responsible not only for Meads' broken arm but the shattered thumb Lochore suffered in the Australian test in 1968. In Australia he was in possession, but in a smothering tackle. As Lochore came to him in support Kirton worked his elbows vigorously to free the ball and one elbow wrenched Lochore's thumb from its socket, splintering it in the process. "At Springs, in that bitch of a game, I went down in a bloody maelstrom of swishing boots. Pinetree was there in a flash, flung himself across me and yelled, 'It's OK; I've got you.' He was protecting me from the boots and copped one himself. He came to me a little later holding his arm. He said, 'The bloody thing's numb. There's no feeling in the fingers.' That sounded all bad to me."

The saga of Pinetree Meads' broken arm is well enough known. That he returned to play five successive matches before the third test was some sort of eighth wonder. But it also invited scrutiny of the selection process. When Meads returned to play it was while wearing a protective leather sleeve on the arm. That he was not as effective as a player was plain. But was he more effective within that limitation than others? Lochore says he has no problem with the selection of Meads for the third test. "A lot of people have given us hell over the decision to play a man with a broken arm but in the end we would not have played him had he rejected the possibility. The selection panel thought it important to have him on the field if he was able. After that the consideration had to be whether he was better at 90 per cent than another at 110 per cent.

"We considered him to be the best available lock. There is a perception that he was rushed into the test. In fact, he had played five straight games before it so it was not as if we lacked opportunity to judge him. Experience will tell you that some players cope with pain better than others. Some with minor injuries must leave the field. Others with considerable injuries can play through the pain, challenging it almost."

Meads says that in some ways it was unfortunate he was made

vice-captain of the team. He concedes selection balance on tour might have been better achieved had Laidlaw or MacRae been appointed. He doubts the selections would have changed much but believes there might have been "more harmonious acceptance of them". Of his own selection for the third test, he says he was very conscious that having played five matches in a row before the test he was the cause of some resentment among other players. "I could understand that. It was one of those things which can cause a rift in a team. The arm was still not right and I knew it but I also knew there was pressure on me to play in the test. It came especially from Ivan and, frankly, it wasn't in me to turn my back on him. It was 'the team needs you' sort of thing. Other than in the lineouts I did not play well and afterward I felt I had let the team down by playing."

Lochore adds that the tour unveiled more fluctuations in the form of individuals than any other tour of his experience and that this, added to injuries and sickness, made a tightrope of selection. "People back home were asking why we kept changing the team. But I can say in hindsight there is only one test selection I would change. With Chris Laidlaw in hospital and Sid Going nursing injury I am damned sure we should have played Fergie McCormick at halfback in the final test. We lacked the courage to do it. We were overly concerned with his state of body and mind after the hammering he had taken in the third test.

"I know now Fergie would have lapped it up, anything to get in there and compete. And the fact is that with his strength and natural skills and his competitiveness he would not have been out of place at all. The Boks knew Sid couldn't run so they put pressure on our midfield where we were without Wayne Cottrell who was a superb player on that tour."

While the tour unleashed on to the rugby world a phenomenal young player like Bryan Williams, it was on the absence from it of an old hand that Lochore believes the fate of the series swung. "When Ken Gray chose not to tour it created an ominous gap where we knew we had to be exceptionally strong. Ken pulled out on moral grounds and I had the greatest respect for his motives. It is no exaggeration to say that the Springboks would have had no answer to him, that he would have dominated short ball at the lineouts and that his method of scrummaging would not have been countered. His lineout option could very well have swung the series."

Recognising there was unrest in the ranks over selection decisions, over test losses and of perceived inadequacies in training and of management, Lochore states the ingredients were there for the tour to fall apart. Had it not been for the cushion of experience placed between team and management by himself and Meads with the support of Vodanovich, had it not been that they had the respect of the players, the tour could have splintered irreparably.

It was a surprising frailty in a country as strongly tuned to the practicalities of rugby that, no matter a manager's inexperience of the playing of the game, he was a tour selector. "Managers with the rugby background of Kilby and Saxton had wisdom to offer in selection but there were others in whom the power to select was misplaced – not their fault, but a serious flaw in the system. You cannot have shallow selections on tour – that is, selections pushed without knowledge of the requirements of positions nor of the need for development of combinations and of tactics for each opposition."

Lochore's thumbnail assessment of the series is of inadequacy in the first test; an outstanding performance in the second which, after two tries had been disallowed, was won only by a penalty goal late in the game; a bad performance in the third; a comprehensively "winning" performance in all things but the result in the fourth.

"The rugby of South Africa has nationalism at its roots. They're incredibly good planners, disciplinarians, pugnaciously determined, obstinate. They carry out their instructions. They breed great slabs of men and they become rugby players as a fact of life. They are more determined, even than us, to win. They pull themselves tightly together as representatives of their country. There's an unshakable pride in what they are — and that may be the way in which they are most like us. Playing at home they are in defence of their nation, their land. On tour they do not retain the fervour and they become vulnerable. They are 25 per cent harder to beat at home than here.

"Of all South Africans the one I would say most epitomises my vision of the Springbok would be the loose forward Piet Greyling, for his total, unbending commitment to their cause. But you could talk in the same breath of John Gainsford, Joggie Jansen, Dawie de Villiers, Lionel Wilson . . . the South Africans' understanding of rugby is vast. In 1970 we did not respect them enough in anticipation of the tour. Perhaps that was a hangover from 1965. In 1970 we did not have respect for them comparable with what we had for the French in 1967 and that was inexcusable. It meant that our planning and our mental preparation were less acute than they should have been.

"I came to better understand them as rugby people in 1971 when I played with de Villiers, Jansen, Frik du Preez and Hannes Marais in the World team which helped England celebrate its rugby centenary. They are such intense students of the game. Playing with them taught me a hell of a lot. There I was, a year after the tour, with greater respect for them than when we were planning to play them. Pinetree felt much the same. I gained great respect for de Villiers, for his on-field organisation. We were throwing everything into the pot; South African moves, New Zealand moves, French moves . . . communication was brilliant and we beat England at Twickenham to wind the whole show up."

More enlightened about the Springboks he might have been, fired-up, indeed, by the experience in England where he played as well as ever he had, but when Lochore came home to Hastwell it was to self-judgement. From the farmhouse he points across the road to a paddock. "It was there. I was browsing with the sheep in the sun and I started thinking about rugby and about myself. A Lions tour coming up, Lochore nudging 31. What did I feel? Was there the tightening in the gut in anticipation of the Lions? Was I one hundred per cent committed to getting on with it again? And I knew I wasn't.

"So was it fair to other players – and to myself – to hang on for the sake of hanging on? It was as if rugby was becoming a habit. I came straight back over here and told Pam I was retiring. One week before – one day before – I had no intention of retiring. I suppose I could have shammed my way through because I was playing well but I would have known. That would have been impossible for me to deal with."

It's a funny thing, retirement. Even farmers retiring only from rugby can stretch, contemplate time and space, more golf, more tennis. But there seem always to be glitches in the retirement system and if you happen to be a recently retired All Black captain, retirement can be hazardous, indeed. A couple of weeks before the Lions were to play the third test at Wellington they played Wairarapa-Bush at Masterton. Lochore received a stricken call from the coach, Ivan Aitkenhead. He had lost Ian Turley and had no player of comparable size to replace him. Would Lochore please just consider it? "I didn't want to play but the fear of letting people down nagged at me and I agreed. I played at lock and played pretty well and we gave the Lions a fair run. For me it was a breeze without captaincy concerns. I got to where the play was, jumped in the lineouts. It was almost a throwback to the early 1960s when I was making my way, doing my own thing. At the end of it I was happy I'd played and happy enough that my final game of rugby had been where it all started." The Friday lunchtime before the Wellington test, Bob Duff, the New Zealand captain of 1956 and now a selector, rang Lochore. "We have here an emergency. Peter Whiting is not able to play, Colin Meads and Ian Kirkpatrick are doubtful starters. We need a lock, but if neither Colin nor Kirky can play we also need someone who can captain the team. You are the only player who can do the job. Will you play?"

Lochore was dubious. He discussed options. But Duff was adamant that he was the only possible option. "We need you; we really need you," he said. And Lochore knew he had no choice. He chucked some gear in a bag, wrote a note for Pam saying, "Gone to Wellington. Playing test tomorrow", drove the Land-Rover to the station and caught the train to Wellington. "If I could have been sure no other New Zealander would ever have known I had been asked, I probably would have declined. But I could never place myself in a position where it appeared I had let the country down. I have always been disappointed it was never fully explained to the media why I came back for one game. It was not just because they needed a lock to replace Whiting. It was because of the other uncertainties with Pinetree and Kirky. I am not disappointed I played. I suppose I was no better and no worse than any other player that day. It was a poor New Zealand performance. I played in the middle of the lineout, marking Gordon Brown I think. It was not the sort of preparation anyone would want for a test. I didn't have a run with the team. As with my first against England in 1964, so with the last in 1971.

"It seemed everyone else in New Zealand had a hang-up about my coming back. I was criticised at least equally with the selectors. It was not a matter of whether I wanted to play or just decided to play, it was that I was needed to play. The general charge was that I did myself a disservice but what I was doing to myself was the least of my considerations. How could I possibly have lived with myself knowing I had been approached to help New Zealand in an emergency and had turned my back? I was as depressed in that defeat as in any other. It was a depression deepened because I wished I had had the time to prepare myself, to plan for my opponent, to feel part of a team.

"Of all the challenges I took up in my life as a player this probably was the greatest. I do not regret confronting it. I regret bitterly only that I was not better prepared for it."

PART TWO
GARY CAFFELL

5

THE MIRACLE MAN

Seated in Invercargill's Rugby Park grandstand on a still-wintry October day, Brian Lochore was feeling decidedly uneasy. His Wairarapa-Bush team had a strong wind in their favour in this all-important match but, with halftime almost upon them, were three points down . . . and playing badly.

Lochore could understand why. Tough games against Taranaki and South Canterbury in the finals of the North Island and national second division competitions within the past seven days were taking their toll.

Physically strong but mentally tired, his players were struggling to get themselves out of second gear and the prospects of beating Southland and winning promotion to the first division were slipping away.

Never a pessimist, even Lochore was starting to think that victory was, at best, a remote possibility.

In his pre-match build-up he had stressed the need for his side to take command within those first forty minutes. He had told them the wind was worth 12 points and that a halftime lead of anything less would not be good enough, especially against a Southland team with players of the calibre of All Blacks Ken Stewart, Brian McKechnie and Steve Pokere.

At the interval, with Wairarapa-Bush still 6-9 down, Lochore knew he had to take an entirely different tack from that followed in two seasons in charge of Wairarapa-Bush. He had no option but to bawl them out.

Lochore does not enjoy the memory; not because he was in the hot seat but because of the strong bond which had been built up between players and management.

"It was terribly, terribly hard," Lochore recalls. "We had come a long way in a short time and a lot of it was due to the spirit existing within the squad. We had spent two years building confidence and self belief amongst the players and now I had to go down there and read the riot act. I knew full well shock tactics were required but the thought of doing it didn't exactly thrill me."

That halftime address by Lochore is now part of Wairarapa-Bush rugby folklore.

Lochore can't remember exactly what he said but the message was crystal clear. "It was one of the most difficult things I've ever done in rugby," he says. "I had to make them look at themselves, to realise that their whole season depended on the forty minutes to come. I think I might have even used the word gutless to describe how they were playing and that hurt considering I knew damn well what they were going through."

Captain of that Wairarapa-Bush team Gary McGlashan, who chalked up more than a hundred games for the union, remembers the players being "shocked to buggery" by Lochore's outburst.

"It was the first time any of us had heard BJ blow his top," McGlashan says. "We were used to him coming onto the paddock and talking to us in a very controlled, quiet sort of manner, just pointing out a few things we needed to do or brush up on. But this time he really let rip. It was a good old bollocking and it really shook us up. He used words he had never used in front of us before and the effect was pretty amazing. We couldn't get back into it quick enough."

Southland had their own ideas, of course. With McKechnie from first five-eighth using the wind intelligently, the home side were on hard attack for most of the first twenty minutes of the second half but, frustratingly, the points didn't come.

Lochore says the ferocity of the Wairarapa-Bush defence in that period was vital to the end result. "Southland threw everything at us but we just made tackle after tackle. You wouldn't get a gutsier effort anywhere. It was incredible stuff. And the longer we held them out the more mistakes they started to make. In the end we won by scoring a great try but really it was our defence in that twenty minutes which did the trick."

The try which took Wairarapa Bush into the first division was a spectacular affair and a carbon copy of many they had scored over the season. Southland were caught totally by surprise when Wairarapa-Bush started a movement from well inside their own half and with backs and forwards combining set up number eight Carl Baker for the dash to the tryline. Wairarapa-Bush were ahead 10-9 and nothing was going to relieve them of their advantage.

For Lochore the emotion of that 1981 win over Southland and promotion to the first division has been matched in his coaching career only by the thrill of taking the All Blacks to their win in the inaugural World Cup.

"Quite honestly the two of them would be on a par," he says. "I know people from the bigger centres might struggle to understand that but for Wairarapa-Bush to get to first division . . . well, considering our lack of population and consequently our lack of playing numbers, it was a staggering achievement. Not so much for me personally but for the players, the officials, the supporters . . . everyone. It was the sort of feeling we'd never experienced before and everybody was just so rapt about it."

Rapt would be putting it mildly. And it is not the actual win over Southland which sticks most in the memory but what followed.

First there was the plane trip home from the deep south. Men like Lochore and Andy Earl, then just a youngster but later an All Black, could never be accused of being softies but they were foremost amongst those who took on a ghostlike appearance as Wellington Airport neared, the aircraft rocking and swaying in the blustery wind. Sobering for sure!

Once safely in Wellington there was the bus journey home. The boys were happy and a stop-off at a well-known Featherston hotel was a must. There was no hurry. The success of the previous day could be savoured at leisure. Or could it? Not long after the team reached Featherston there was a phone call. A welcoming ceremony has been arranged in Masterton, 42 kilometres up the road, and the team was wanted there pronto. Nothing to be too worried about though. Just a few people wanting to shake hands and then the celebrations could continue.

Wrong again! As the bus carrying the team reached Masterton and wove its way towards the War Memorial Stadium it became clear this was something out of the ordinary. Hundreds, thousands, of people crowded the streets. It seemed like the whole of Masterton's 19,000-plus population, and then some, were there.

For many of the players it was the most emotional moment of their sporting lives. Veteran campaigners like Bill Rowlands, Neil Kjestrup and McGlashan had put their bodies on the line for Wairarapa-Bush time and time again and until now had never really been thanked for it. They couldn't believe it.

As the players left the bus and made their way to the area where the official speeches were to be made there was a roar which would have done credit to a match-winning try in a Ranfurly Shield match. And as each player was introduced the roar became more and more deafening. Nobody was greeted louder than Lochore, "the miracle man" as one local identity described him. That day he was God, or as close to it as anybody could hope to get.

But how many people who celebrated Wairarapa-Bush's success and who sang Lochore's praises remembered back to the end of the 1978 season when he first made himself available as selector-coach for the union.

Considering that Wairarapa-Bush had secured just two wins from twelve games the previous year under coach Rod McKenzie, Lochore, taking into account his outstanding playing record, both for Wairarapa and New Zealand, should have been a shoo in. Amazingly, McKenzie retained the job, with the *Wairarapa Times-Age* recording that "the reappointment decision prompted little discussion from management committee members and McKenzie was re-elected after getting more than 51 per cent on the first vote".

Typically, Lochore was unfazed at his failure to get the nod. He recalls being asked to stand for the post and with the team struggling to make any sort of impact against even the lesser-rated provincial sides thought he could be of some assistance, "if they wanted me".

"Wairarapa rugby had been good to me in my playing days and this seemed to be a way of giving something back to them. But quite honestly I didn't lose any sleep over missing out. In fact, it was probably a good thing for even had I got it there were obviously some union officials who didn't want me. The last thing a coach needs is divisions of that nature."

International referee Bob Francis, a member of the Wairarapa-Bush union at the time, believes parochialism could have played a part in Lochore's fate as to some people he was still identified as a player and coach with the Masterton club, roles from which he had retired some years earlier.

"There was a fair bit of feeling between clubs in those days and that could have had something to do with it," Francis says. "But at the same time they didn't sack coaches as easily then as they do now. You tended to take the view that the incumbent had to be given a fair go."

As it happened, Wairarapa-Bush fared even worse in 1979 than they had in 1978, managing just one win and a draw from their eleven games. Again Lochore was asked to make himself available for the coaching job. With a "little prompting" he again allowed his name to go forward.

"I guess it was a case of not wanting to give the impression there was any sour grapes on my part about missing out the year before. I still thought I had something to offer and so I stood again. But that was it, I wouldn't have gone a third time," he says.

Come the 1980 season, Lochore's aspirations for the

Wairarapa-Bush side were relatively simple. Considering the lack of success in recent times he was not anticipating anything special from them, especially since the confidence of the players was at a low ebb.

"Confidence is such a big thing in rugby and in Wairarapa-Bush we had reached the stage where the players had very little left. We had to go back to square one and slowly but surely get their confidence to the point where they could go onto the paddock, enjoy their rugby and perhaps pick up a win or two along the way."

Wairarapa-Bush's first game under Lochore was an early-season pipe-opener against Wellington and while the coach was diligent in terms of tactical preparation he forgot to mention one thing – dress code. Lochore – ever a believer that a team which dresses well plays well – was shocked when his players turned up for the game in open necked shirts and jeans, looking "like a motley lot of country bumpkins".

"I bit my tongue and said nothing on the day but next training I laid down the law as far as dress, both before and after matches, was concerned. The look of shock on some of their faces when I said they had to wear ties . . . they couldn't believe it. But they had them on for the next game, even if some of the knots were not exactly tied to perfection!"

Lochore remembers the players becoming so proud of their dress code that towards the end of the season, when a new player was brought into the squad at the eleventh hour and turned up for the game in casual attire, he was quietly taken aside by a senior team member and told to find himself a tie. "I knew then we were on the right track," he laughs.

In terms of results, the 1980 season was better, much better, than even the most ardent Wairarapa-Bush supporter could have expected. In eleven games there were six wins and a draw and third placing in the North Island second division.

"The big thing was that we had got ourselves a base from which we could work towards improving even further the next season. We had built up a strong spirit within the squad and everybody was on the same level. We had become a team in the true sense of the word and that's important, especially in smaller unions where the odds are often stacked against you. Everybody has to jell together in that environment," Lochore says.

Flushed by the progress made by their team under Lochore, the Wairarapa-Bush union had no hesitation returning him as selector-coach for 1981. It was to be a season of seasons in the history of the union but, at the outset, Lochore was guarded in his aims for a team still young and relatively inexperienced in the ways of top level rugby.

Mindful of the fact that size was always going to be a problem among his forwards and that speed around the paddock would be an absolute necessity if they were to be competitive, he encouraged his players to follow fitness programmes over the summer months. "I said to the guys that if they weren't going to be the biggest team about, they had to be the fittest. That was something which was in their own hands and to their credit they really worked at it. We didn't meet many teams who matched us in that regard," Lochore says.

By having his players enjoy social occasions together from time to time the team spirit was further enhanced. Doug Bracewell, brother of international cricketers John and Brendan and a former Central Districts cricket representative himself, was one of the new faces introduced by Lochore to the Wairarapa-Bush side in 1980 and he recalls the impact Lochore had, not only on his players but their whole families.

"Brian always stressed the importance of the families being aware of what you as a player were doing, of what you were trying to achieve," Bracewell says. "Even at training sessions the wives were quite welcome to come along and it actually got to the stage where they were encouraging their husbands to go to practice, to give a hundred per cent and more to the team. They wanted us to do well, every bit as much as we did ourselves. It was a very happy unit and I think that showed through on the field of play."

Among Wairarapa-Bush's early matches of 1981 was one against neighbouring Manawatu, then a first division team as powerful as any in the country. It was always going to be a tough assignment but few expected Wairarapa-Bush to be on the end of a 51-6 hiding.

But the coach was not unhappy and considered it a vital component in the success which emerged as the season unfolded. Lochore's view was that Manawatu had played the type of rugby which Wairarapa-Bush had often talked about trying to play themselves; rugby which involved the dominance of second-phase possession and quick and accurate movement of the ball.

"It was the best practical demonstration a coach could ever hope his team to get. From there on, instead of having to explain what I wanted I could relate things back to that particular match and the players knew exactly what I was getting at. They had to become as desperate as Manawatu in their pursuit of the ball and as efficient as them in distributing and using it. The challenge was there and they had to respond to it."

A hiding of the magnitude handed out by Manawatu could, of course, have tempted many coaches to make wholesale changes to personnel but, as Gary McGlashan recalls, players operating under Lochore's command could rely on his loyalty, even if they had a bad game.

"With BJ you knew you had the confidence of the coach, that it wasn't a matter of one poor game and you're out. There was always a second chance and the players appreciated the feeling of security that gave them."

Doug Bracewell remembers with fondness as an inside back the fact that Lochore, a forward himself, went out of his way to ensure that the backs were treated as equals. "He showed a lot more subtlety about back play than most coaches of his time. He was always looking for us to play an expansive style of game and that made not only the game itself, but training, enjoyable. We were forever moving the ball wide and trying new things. It was refreshing and we loved it. There were a lot of times when we didn't want training to stop."

That the team were enjoying what they were doing was brilliantly illustrated on the field of play. With the Manawatu defeat behind them, Wairarapa-Bush started to hit their straps.

Sparkling tries became second nature as the team registered seven successive wins and presented themselves with the chance of winning the North Island second division, the national second division title and promotion to first division.

More than anything else, it was the one-week time frame which worried Lochore in regard to his players successfully achieving all three objectives. He was confident they now had the belief in themselves to perform well against any opposition but expecting them to play the divisional equivalent of three test matches in seven days was surely asking the impossible.

"It was a crazy programme, especially for a union our size and with our playing resources, but we had no alternative but to tackle it head on. The pressure on the players was enormous and, quite frankly, I couldn't see them getting through it. The mental exhaustion alone would surely be too much for them to handle," he says.

The North Island second division championship was finalised before a capacity crowd at Masterton's Memorial Park, with a Taranaki side spearheaded by All Blacks Graham Mourie and Dave Loveridge hot favourites to win. Lochore was aware of what individuals of this calibre were capable and he devised plans aimed at nullifying their impact.

"We knew that Taranaki would revolve a lot of their play around Mourie and Loveridge and so we concentrated on running as much ball as we could straight at them so as to take them out of the game," Lochore says. "We figured the more time we had them on the ground the better for us and that's the way things worked out."

Gary McGlashan considers the 15-6 win over Taranaki as the most exciting game in his entire career. "We really rose to the crowd that day," he recalls. "They got right behind us and there was so much noise it made the hairs stand up on the back of my neck. We daren't lose with that sort of support behind us."

Taranaki, winners over both Auckland and Wellington in lead-up games to the second division series, were unprepared for Wairarapa-Bush's willingness to attack them from all parts of the paddock. Possession was about evenly shared from the forward exchanges but Wairarapa-Bush were much more inventive in their back play and continually confused the Taranaki defensive screen with swift changes of direction and aggressive running.

Lochore still smiles at a question put to him by Wairarapa-Bush chairman David Galvin in the days leading up to the game. "He asked me if I thought the union should book our seats on the plane to Invercargill just in case we got that far. I told him not to worry, that Taranaki would already have booked and we'd just take their bookings. And that's exactly what happened."

Lochore also recalls from the Taranaki game a classic illustration of the spirit built up between players and management. When veteran prop forward Bill Rowlands tore his shorts there were none to fit him among those in the gear bag. Rather than let Rowlands see out the match with torn shorts, Graham Humphrey, who managed Wairarapa-Bush throughout Lochore's reign as selector-coach, left the ground and went to a residence in town where he located a pair of the right size.

"Humph missed a good deal of the second half in doing it but that's the sort of manager he was," Lochore said. "The players always came first."

After the Taranaki victory, Wairarapa-Bush had to face South Island second division champions South Canterbury at Masterton before any trip to Invercargill could be confirmed. Lochore admits to concern about the possibility of Wairarapa-Bush suffering a let-down. To some extent that did occur but Wairarapa-Bush were still good enough to take the game by a decisive margin.

Lochore was mindful of the need to freshen his team in the

hope they would find the levels of energy necessary to cope with a Southland team whose preparation for the promotion-relegation match had been much more relaxed.

"There was no point in doing any hard training at all between the South Canterbury and Southland games," Lochore says. "I remember we had a game of basketball at Kuranui College in Greytown on the way to Wellington Airport and then just a light training run at Invercargill on the Friday. And that was just to get the players up mentally rather than do anything from a physical viewpoint."

On reflection, Lochore agrees the experience of coaching Wairarapa-Bush through those memorable seven days stood him in good stead when he took charge of the All Blacks and found them in similar situations, particularly during their 1987 World Cup campaign. "It certainly taught me a lot in regards to preparing any side from a psychological viewpoint. You can't keep pushing players, either physically or mentally, because in the end something will give. You have to keep them as fresh as you can so that when they go onto the paddock they are keen and alert with everything functioning at one hundred per cent. Anything less and you can't expect a maximum performance; the human body just doesn't work that way."

Lochore says that as a coach he has always placed faith in each player's ability to get themselves to the point where they were ready to fire on match day. "If part of their preparation was having a beer or two on a Friday night then so be it. That was OK with me providing it had no effect on their performance on the field of play."

Wairarapa-Bush's stirring second half revival to win in Invercargill was celebrated by the rugby community as a whole. A win for the little guy helped restore people's faith in rugby, battered by the effects of the Springbok tour that year, and the nation rejoiced with them.

Rugby News editor Bob Howitt described Wairarapa-Bush's advance to the big time as a "great inspiration". "Not too many mice come to roar in the rugged New Zealand representative rugby jungle so there's a certain romance attached to those who do," he wrote in surmising that Wairarapa-Bush must have been at 250 to one at the start of the season to win the North Island second division title, let alone contemplate the giddy heights of promotion to first division. "They have won the hearts of New Zealand rugby followers everywhere. New Zealanders love to champion the underdog and that's Wairarapa-Bush's role right now."

But it went further than that. As Bob Francis – later to become Mayor of Masterton – says, even non-rugby people in the Wairarapa-Bush area were suddenly talking rugby and it brought a new-found unity to a region which had been having its share of financial and social difficulties. "It was amazing. Everywhere you went the conversation soon got round to rugby. You'd get old ladies up the street talking about it even though they'd never been near a game themselves."

And for Wairarapa-Bush administrators it was the start of an era which saw their headquarters at Memorial Park upgraded and organisation improved.

"I think that as administrators we knew we were in the midst of something special and that we had to make the most of it. It was a very exciting time for Wairarapa-Bush rugby," Francis says. "It was probably similar to what happened when Marlborough took the Ranfurly Shield in the early 1970s. The flow-on effects were something to behold."

Francis also believes that Lochore was the ideal man to have at the helm; that a lesser person might have been swept away by the adulation accorded both him and his team. "One of the great traits of BJ is that he can relate to anyone in the community, from the man sweeping the streets to the bank manager. There is never anything false about him and people in smaller areas like Wairarapa-Bush respond to that sort of leadership. To them BJ was just BJ, nothing more, nothing less. No matter how well the team performed they knew he wouldn't change, that he would have his feet firmly placed on the ground."

As Francis points out, it has not only been in rugby where Lochore's impact on the Wairarapa-Bush region has been immense. "He's given a lot to the community in general as well," he says. "He's one of those special people who have leadership qualities which stretch far beyond just one aspect of their life. His influence outside rugby has been just as strong as it has been within it."

Education is one area in which Lochore's influence has been considerable. He spent some time as chairman of the board of his old secondary school, Wairarapa College, and when another secondary institution, Kuranui College in Greytown, was having problems which saw their board of trustees sacked by the Minister of Education, Lockwood Smith, it was Lochore who was appointed as commissioner to oversee the running of the school until the problems could be solved. It was typical of Lochore's willingness to accept and deliver on a challenge that for a period of about 14 months he spent at least a day a week at Kuranui helping to get the school back on an even keel.

Lochore said the Kuranui experience undoubtedly ranked as one of his greatest challenges outside rugby. "The invitation came right out of the blue and I must admit I didn't really know what I was getting into. But I reckoned that if I could give some assistance to a community within Wairarapa in distress then I would," he recalls.

Essentially, the sacking of the board came because factions had developed and there was little or no unanimity in their decision-making. It was a traumatic time for staff, parents and pupils and Lochore concedes that his appointment as commissioner was treated with suspicion, particularly by staff. "There didn't seem to be too much animosity from parents and pupils but I think some of the staff saw me as a stooge for Lockwood Smith; that I was there with some sort of political agenda."

Lochore says with a commissioner having the power to hire

and fire staff he could understand the reluctance of the teachers to welcome him with open arms. "It was never on my mind to get into the business of sacking staff but I guess they never knew that," he says. "So it was important that we got together as soon as possible and I could tell them exactly where I was coming from."

At a meeting with Kuranui staff, Lochore told them that they had to accept him "warts and all". He stressed he was not working under any political banner, that he was there to do what he saw as best for the college, that it was vital that everybody within the school community started working in harmony so that any previous divisions became a thing of the past.

"The stage had been reached where because of the debate which was going on from day to day – much of it in the local press – parents were expressing their views to their children and the kids were then taking them to school. And, of course, the staff were having their say as well," Lochore remembers. "It was a total mess and it was pretty obvious that if those sort of things weren't arrested and attitudes changed then the future of the college itself was in question. That's how serious things were."

Lochore said that much of his time at Kuranui was spent talking to pupils, staff and parents, emphasising ground rules which had to be followed, whether they liked it or not.

"It was important that everybody knew what was right and what was wrong. We all had to be heading in the same direction otherwise we would have got nowhere," Lochore says. "The main aim was to instil a sense of confidence and pride into everybody associated with the college and eventually we managed to do that."

Lochore says he was delighted that, when the time was ripe for him to stand aside and a new board of trustees elected, eight people offered themselves for the five positions. "That was very encouraging," he says. "It had taken a while but finally we had reached the stage where people were prepared to come forward and run the school the way it should be run."

Brian Lochore's sporting involvement in the Wairarapa extended beyond rugby. Tennis and golf have been two activities which have commanded his attention on a regular basis over the summer months with tennis providing him with one of his fondest sporting memories.

Lochore was a member of the Wairarapa senior tennis team which in January 1982 pulled off a stunning upset by beating Manawatu 18-6 to win the Christie Cup, symbol of supremacy among the sub-associations of the lower North Island, for the first time in 43 years. The input of Lochore into that victory was considerable as he won all three of his games.

"It was a big moment for Wairarapa tennis and it was great to be part of it," Lochore says. "It was a lot like what happened with the rugby team actually as we had reached the stage as a unit where we were ready to do something special. If it didn't happen then it was never going to happen."

Wairarapa-Bush's debut season in rugby's premier league had arrived and with it a feeling throughout the sport that they would do well to survive. Lochore had other ideas. He was quietly confident he had the players to respond to the greater challenge providing they did not place themselves under too much pressure.

"We had to be very careful about setting ourselves goals, of not aiming too high," he says. "We had to take just one game at a time and not worry about what had happened before and what might happen later. The focus had to be entirely on the game in hand."

Before the New Zealand season got under way, Wairarapa-Bush took up an invitation from the Queensland Rugby Union to play a match against the state side at Ballymore. It was Michael Lynagh's first game for Queensland and although Wairarapa-Bush were on the end of a decent beating they won the hearts of the locals with their never-say-die attitude.

"They gave us a bit of a bath in the first half but we actually scored more points than them in the second. We came home pretty proud of what we had achieved," Lochore says. "Just being invited to play at Ballymore was a huge fillip for a union our size. I guess it showed we had arrived!"

Wairarapa-Bush's opening first division games saw them pitted against traditional sparring partners Wellington and Hawke's Bay followed by a northern tour taking in matches against North Auckland, Auckland and Waikato.

Wellington were the Ranfurly Shield holders when they arrived in Masterton and they had travelled over the Rimutaka Hills chockful of confidence that victory was simply a matter of course. It wasn't long into the game, however, before the Wellington players got the message that Wairarapa-Bush had no intention of being easy-beats.

In a nine-all draw, All Black fullback Allan Hewson kicked three penalties for the visitors – accused by coach Ian Upston of playing "like girls" – while Wairarapa-Bush managed a converted try and a dropped goal. It was as good a start as Wairarapa-Bush could have hoped for but their delight was tempered when in the next championship game they were on the end of a comprehensive 21-3 beating by Hawke's Bay.

The northern tour began with North Auckland rolling out the welcome mat and then blitzing Wairarapa-Bush 28-3.

It was now time for Lochore to make a decision. Did he field a first string line-up against the mighty Auks or was he prepared to risk a huge defeat by giving his reserves a much-needed run? Lochore didn't hesitate. Always a believer in keeping all members of a team as fully employed as possible, he chose in favour of the reserves and Auckland romped home 46-6.

"Looking back I suppose we could have kept the score down a bit by playing a full-strength side but that would have meant some players not getting a run on tour and I couldn't accept that," Lochore says. "To me, having 21 happy players has always been better than having 15 happy players and six who are not."

Other aspects of Lochore's man-management skills came to the fore after the Eden Park defeat. Aware his players were down in the dumps his preparation for the Waikato match four days later was deliberately low key. So low key, in fact, that pupils and staff at one of the country's most famous rugby schools, St Stephen's College, must have wondered what on earth was going on.

The Wairarapa-Bush squad was invited to train there and a good-sized crowd gathered to watch Lochore at work. If they expected to see something special they were to be disappointed. The Wairarapa-Bush team spent most of the time trying out their soccer skills and when they did run as a team Lochore had the backs working as forwards and the forwards as backs.

Comments had been overheard among the players after the Auckland match, comments which suggested that the forwards might not have been pushing as hard as they might in the scrums. Not surprisingly, it was the backs who were making the noise, even if it was of a playful nature, and so Lochore decided to give them a taste of what the forwards faced.

"It probably wasn't what those watching expected but to me it was the good of the team which had to come first," Lochore recalls of that St Stephen's training session. "They had taken a couple of decent beatings but I was happy enough with the way they had played and felt the last thing they needed was a hard work-out. It was more important to get their spirits up, to get them smiling again."

A team training followed on the Thursday at Hamilton and then on the Friday Lochore surprised his players by telling them he would not be conducting a training session himself that day and that the players could please themselves how they filled in their time.

Again there was good reason behind Lochore's thinking. "Somewhere along the line players have to take responsibility for their own actions," he says. "There is only so much a coach can do; at the end of the day it's the players who have to get out there and do the business."

The Wairarapa-Bush players responded in the manner in

which Lochore thought they would. A team meeting was called by senior members and a decision was made to run a training session themselves. The seeds for an upset win over Waikato had been well and truly sown.

The Hamilton game was a thriller with Waikato threatening to dominate through their forwards before Wairarapa-Bush lifted themselves in the second half and snatched a deserved 19-15 win. Lochore and his team were rapt that success at first division level had finally been achieved with the coach taking particular pleasure that it had been managed away from home.

"Winning in a place like Hamilton had to be a major confidence booster for the players," he said. "There's always something about taking on the locals and beating them in front of their home crowd. It tends to give you an extra lift."

After Waikato came a 12-11 loss to Counties and then a 16-3 win over Bay of Plenty which, if not providing a spectacle of any moment, was a big step towards Wairarapa-Bush retaining first division status. When Otago came to Masterton and were beaten 12-10, after leading 10-0 at one stage, first division tenure was assured.

Manawatu was next with Wairarapa-Bush beaten 24-14. In a game which saw a couple of key Wairarapa-Bush players injured, the usually diplomatic Lochore was prompted to comment that his team had been dealt out "some pretty ordinary stuff".

Then it was on to Christchurch for a match against Canterbury which doubled as a Ranfurly Shield fixture. An army of supporters was present to back the Wairarapa-Bush side but a team depleted by injuries was never in the hunt and was thumped 51-6.

Doug Bracewell recalls that game not because of the final scoreline but because of the positive manner in which Lochore prepared his team. "It was typical of Brian," Bracewell says. "He could instil the sort of self-belief into players that made them think they could do anything, that no team was unbeatable no matter what the odds. I remember us going to Christchurch convinced that we were in with a chance. But despite the fact we got stuck in and shook them up for a while we didn't have the resources to last the whole eighty minutes."

The saddest thing about that loss, however, was not the size of the defeat but that it was the swansong of Brian Lochore as Wairarapa-Bush coach. The reasons were twofold. First and foremost was the feeling in Lochore's mind that after three years it was time for a change.

"I've always thought that coaching comes in three-year cycles," he says. "The first year is spent doing the groundwork, the second you look to improve your performance and be better organised and in the third year you harvest what you have sown. After that it all becomes a bit repetitive, especially if the playing personnel stays about the same."

Lochore was happy, too, in the knowledge that whoever took over from him in 1983 would have a team experienced in the ways of first division rugby and confident in their ability to perform well at the highest levels.

"Things were nicely settled, it was as good a time as any to bring someone new in," he says. Lochore's point was proved when Wairarapa-Bush, under Lane Penn, remained in first division for four more seasons, including finishing fourth in 1985.

Lochore was under pressure to stand as a member of the All Black selection panel. It had never been an ambition of his to either select or coach on the national stage but with the inevitable publicity which had followed Wairarapa-Bush's rise to premier status had come recognition that Lochore's talents should be retained within the game. Lochore himself was not so sure. "It was like being on a treadmill really," he says. "Here I was finishing one job and another was being put in front of me. It was a case of deciding whether I had the motivation to take the next step and finally I decided I did. But it was never something I sought, not by a long chalk."

The decision to stand down from the Wairarapa-Bush job

brought glowing tributes from both players and officials.

"He had an enormous ability to make players believe in themselves," Gary McGlashan says. "And he was always honest. You knew exactly where you stood with him. A lot of his players took up coaching later on and I'd say most of them tried to follow his principles. There is definitely something special about the man, something that very few people have."

Doug Bracewell says he will always remember the bond between Lochore and his players. "It was built on trust," he said. "We knew that whatever he was doing was for the good of the whole team not just a few individuals. He was always consultative. As players we knew exactly what was going on."

Bracewell considers another key to Lochore's success with Wairarapa-Bush was his selections. "He thought a lot about balance and compatibility. He wanted players who could work well together. And he wasn't afraid to back himself against public opinion. If he thought someone was worth giving a go he gave them a go."

And then there was Lochore's ability to instil discipline amongst his players without ever having to rant and rave. "He always set high standards himself and players soon got to realise that's what he expected of them as well," Bracewell says. "For example, our court sessions had a certain dignity about them. They were witty and humorous rather than just seeing how quickly you could get through a keg."

Graham Humphrey points to communication as one of Lochore's strongpoints. "He always stressed that the interests of the players had to come first, that they had to know exactly what was going on. He never hid anything from them. If he had something to say he said it out in the open for everybody to hear. I think it got to the stage where if they had been asked the players would have walked through fire for him; that's the sort of respect they held for the guy."

Lochore, for his part, takes a somewhat different view of things. He prefers to place the emphasis on how his three-year term as Wairarapa-Bush coach helped him, rather than how he helped his players.

"You wonder what might have happened had not the guys responded so positively to what I was trying to do," he says. "If we had performed badly and made little or no progress, would I have been offered the chance to go any further in the game? In all probability no. So really it's the players who deserve any pat on the back, not me."

From the time he took over Wairarapa-Bush, Lochore followed what he describes as a very simple philosophy on how rugby should be played. "I like to work on the theory that possession is absolutely vital in rugby and that if you don't do something positive with it then you're defeating the purpose of the game, which must be to score tries."

Lochore says too many teams, at both provincial and international level, refuse to run the ball unless they are in, or very close to, opposition territory. He considers this a negative attitude. "If the opportunity is there to run the ball then I've always believed you should run it, no matter where you are in relation to your own goalline," he says. "I hate to see possession kicked away unless there is no other alternative."

His Wairarapa-Bush team worked his system well, Lochore says; that over the three seasons many of their tries came from attacking movements launched from inside their own half.

"Players appreciate the fact that you allow them to take chances, that you say to them that if it's on to attack then attack. It's all a matter of communication; if that's good then you can go from anywhere," he says. "Thinking positive is the key."

Lochore says the importance of team talks should not be under-estimated either. The Wairarapa-Bush experience taught him to carefully plan what he was going to say to his players before each game, something that often involved taking notes so that all avenues which needed to be covered actually were.

But Lochore is no fan of worrying about the tactics which may be used by opposition sides. He considers the main concern for any coach should be to implant their system on the opposition rather than worry about what they might do.

"You often read or hear about coaches who openly express fears about the strength of their opposition. All they're doing is implanting seeds of doubt in the minds of their own players and that's the last thing they need."

And what about the half-time team talk, something which worked the oracle for Wairarapa-Bush in their historic win over Southland in 1981?

Keep them simple, Lochore says, believing that in such a short space of time anything complicated would have little or no effect on the players. "I've always preferred to pick on just one or two things which could be improved. The important thing is to keep the players thinking about the game.

"A lot of games can be won and lost over that five minutes. You can't let your side relax, the pressure has to be maintained. If the players turn off and start thinking about something else then you're in trouble."

Lochore says his stint as Wairarapa-Bush coach helped to strengthen a conviction that the New Zealand Rugby Union must ensure everything possible was done to keep rugby in the smaller unions in a healthy state.

"There are some people in rugby administration who conveniently forget that unions like Wairarapa-Bush are the very grassroots of our game," he says. "Go back thirty years and you will find that many, many of the All Blacks in the period since then have started their rugby in towns like Masterton, Foxton or Methven. They are the breeding grounds for a lot of our top rugby players and always will be. If the sport dies there it will eventually die everywhere."

Lochore believes it vital that players resident in the likes of Wairarapa-Bush are given equal opportunity to play at a higher level and he considers that a competition like the Super 12, contested by regional sides from throughout New Zealand, is a plus in that respect.

"It's certainly a chance for them to get more exposure and to experience probably the next best thing to test match rugby. But the worry is what happens to them if they succeed there. Will they then be swallowed up by the bigger unions with the bigger chequebooks? That's the sort of thing the NZRFU has to address. Rugby needs those players to go back to their grassroots and be inspirations for the kids starting to play the game there."

PART THREE
RON PALENSKI

6

ON THE ROAD AGAIN

For a New Zealand rugby player, South Africa is like the siren song of Greek mythology, the promise of pleasures luring them on. Teams and individuals, like the ancient sailors, have foundered on the rocks but still their successors go back for more.

South Africa is always there as a focal point for New Zealand rugby. It is a goal, a quest. More blood, sweat and tears, plus anguish, heartburn and any other malady of stress and distress, go into a confrontation between New Zealand and South African rugby than any other rugby contest, perhaps any other sporting contest. Other countries have their "auld" and ancient enemies when meetings on the sports fields reflect and remember a history of battles on other fronts; others have their traditional rivals beyond all others who must be dispatched.

New Zealand rugby has South Africa. The political and social effects of some New Zealanders continuing to want to play against apartheid South Africa were both caused by and exacerbated by the underlying rugby feeling that New Zealanders have for South Africa, and South Africans have for New Zealand. In a world that has rapidly changed, and rugby changing dramatically with it, South Africa is a constant. It is always there. The old line about never beating Wales, just scoring more points than them, is true enough but in reality its application to rugby against South Africa holds a more enduring validity.

For Brian Lochore, South Africa always loomed large; as a player, a captain, a coach and as the World Cup campaign manager in 1995. They were the foe who wouldn't go away, the foe who could sometimes be tamed but never caged. And South Africans were the catalyst for Lochore returning to international rugby after he had stopped playing in 1970 and turned to coaching his Masterton club.

In 1979, Lochore had few commitments in rugby other than a deep and abiding interest and a continuing and unquenchable love for the game. And he had no ambitions. Any he had had in rugby were as a player, first to become an All Black and then to be as good an All Black as he could be. The ambitions were achieved way beyond any boy's dreams and Lochore was content that he had done what he had set out to do. His rugby horizon was uncluttered by unfulfilled goals.

It took one phone call to change it. The call was from Robert Denton, an astute and energetic man of South African rugby who was then the executive director of the Northern Transvaal union. Northern Transvaal had just completed extensive remodelling and refurbishing of their Loftus Versfeld ground in Pretoria and, partly to celebrate their centenary and partly to pay off some of the debt, was mounting a tour of South Africa by a World team, tours by any other type of team then being either a political liability or impossibility. Would Lochore, Denton wanted to know, be the coach of the team?

An easy question to ask, a difficult one to answer. This was two years after the Commonwealth heads of governments' Gleneagles Agreement, under which each Commonwealth country was obliged to discourage as much as it could sporting contact with South Africa. There was no legal obligation on any government to ban such contact and, indeed, the agreement specifically provided for the different laws and customs of member countries. The agreement, reached at the Gleneagles Hotel in Scotland at the time of the leaders' summit in London in 1977, came as a direct result of the boycott of the Montreal Olympic Games in 1976 by African, Asian and Caribbean countries in protest against New Zealand not being thrown out of the Games because of the tour that year by the All Blacks of South Africa. Gleneagles was primarily framed to prevent a similar boycott of the Edmonton Commonwealth Games in 1978; which it did.

The world climate was against contact with South Africa such as that being proposed by Robert Denton. The New Zealand climate was more difficult to forecast, largely because rugby against South Africa was a matter of importance to a great many New Zealanders, but a matter of indifference to South Africa's political opponents, especially outside of New Zealand. It was easy for the rest of the world to take a principled stand on something in which it had no direct stake. Very few either inside or outside New Zealand agreed with the root cause of the problem, apartheid, the cynical and outrageous separate "development" by a white minority of South Africa's ethnic groups; the divergence of views came with how best to combat, destroy or dilute it. The New Zealand Government, as it was required to be, was officially against the tour but it would take no direct action against it. The New Zealand Rugby Union, as a body, did not see it as a tour over which it had any control. Its role was to receive and pass on invitations to individual players and its prime concern was that only sanctioned players went and there be a limit to the number of New Zealanders.

None of this applied to Lochore. He was a free agent, answerable to neither the union nor the government. But he was answerable to his conscience.

"I gave it a great deal of thought because of the public debate and the ramifications," he recalled. "I could not give Denton an immediate answer. My view was that it was better to work from within to break down apartheid than from without. I suppose I was one of the bridge-builders rather than the bridge-destroyers. I decided to test how genuine the South African rugby people were and agreed to coach the team provided it was a multiracial team, that we played multiracial teams and that there were no restrictions based on race while we were there. They agreed and my conditions were met. Apartheid still existed officially, of course, but as far as that tour was concerned, rugby circumvented it.

"I don't know if my attitude made any difference at home but I knew I had done my little bit for race relations and I was doing something through sport."

Lochore's decision brought an unusual visit to his Wairarapa farm. He was out working in a paddock at the back of the farm one morning when he noticed a figure in the distance plodding across an adjacent paddock in his direction. From a distance, it wasn't anyone he recognised so, phlegmatically, he carried on with his work till the figure materialised and stated his business. It turned out to be Bill Fleming, the police constable from Eketahuna, the nearest town to the Lochore farm.

"Our police intelligence tells us that there is some danger to your farm while you will be away," he said.

Lochore was staggered and found that hard to believe, but agreed to go along with what the police proposed to do. It was explained that national police headquarters had decided Lochore and each of the New Zealanders going to South Africa should be given watchful protection in case people opposed to the tour decided to take violent action against either property or families left behind.

The plan, the policeman explained, was for three officers from Wellington to base themselves in Eketahuna and cruise out to the Lochore property every so often to ensure that all was well.

This didn't make a lot of sense to Lochore. "Why don't you stay at the house?" he asked. "It's a big house, there's room for you there, all you need do is contribute to the cost of groceries."

National headquarters was consulted and the police moved in. Three of them began the vigil but as time went on and nothing untoward happened, it was reduced to two and, by the end, it was a squad of one. Lochore was away in South Africa for about a month and, evidently, the police presence was neither noticed nor suspected by others in the area. The perceived need for police protection was indicative of the type of feeling in New Zealand at the time, but the under-employment of the officers at the Lochore farm was also indicative that opposition to such tours was neither as determined nor as widespread as may have been supposed. It was, it seemed, essentially city-based opposition and police also kept an eye on each of the players' homes.

The World team tour did not kindle in Lochore any burning ambition to be All Black coach, but it did bring him up to date with international rugby and re-immerse him in its nuances, characteristics and foibles. He had not been involved with any national team for nine years and though he'd followed rugby assiduously, like any other dedicated follower, through newspapers, radio, television and in conversation, the South African tour brought home to him how easy it was to lose touch. He made contact with a new generation of players who had new ways of doing things and new ways of explaining what and why they did it.

"I was not conscious at the time I was getting back into international rugby, but I was conscious of how quickly you can get out of touch with what happens at rugby at the highest level."

Seldom can a rugby coach at international level have had such a polyglot collection of nationalities and abilities under his care. From New Zealand came All Blacks Bill Osborne, Mark Donaldson, Kevin Eveleigh, Andy Haden, Frank Oliver, Gary Knight and Andy Dalton and one of that rarest of New Zealand rugby players, someone who had turned down the chance to be an All Black, Aucklander Greg Denholm.

From Australia, there was veteran lock Garrick Fay, wing Paddy Batch and Greg Cornelsen, a claimant to rugby immortality for scoring four tries against the All Blacks the year before, and also one of rugby's most-liked characters. Rhodesians Ian Robertson, Ray Mordt and Ian Buchanan were there, so were Welshmen Phil Bennett, Jeff Squire and Graham Price. Argentina provided Ricardo Landajo and Tomas Petersen,

Spain Santiago Noriega and Jose Galdos, the United States Denis Jablonski and Jamie Kelleher. From Italy came Rino Francescato and Ambrogio Bona, Hong Kong provided Mike Francis and from South Africa were Thys Laurens and two Coloureds, Errol Tobias, later to be a Springbok, and Hennie Shields.

If the introductions and getting to know such a diverse lot wasn't bad enough for Lochore, he also had to field two teams on the opening day of the tour, one against a Northern Transvaal Invitation XV in the curtain-raiser at Loftus Versfeld and the other against a South African Defence XV in the main event. As any coach will know, selecting and preparing a scratch side for any game is difficult enough, bordering on journeys into the unknown; selecting and coaching two to play on the same day is well over the frontier and deep in uncharted territory. Lochore wisely chose Haden as his first team captain and Oliver as his second, ensuring at least there was hard international experience at the head of each team. Both games were won, which may have been a combination of luck and judgment, and provided Lochore with a chuck-him-in-the-deep-end introduction to international coaching. Lochore also had unhappy memories of an earlier double-up day, when the All Blacks played twice in Perth on the same day in 1970 on the way to South Africa. It was toward the end of the second match that Lochore broke a bone in a hand, keeping him out of the first five games in South Africa.

Lochore in 1979 also had to contend, though at a distance, with an unholy row raging in New Zealand about the propriety of two of the players, Eveleigh and Denholm, being in South Africa at all. They had been invited by Northern Transvaal but their invitations had not been approved by the New Zealand union, and the union and anti-apartheid lobbyists found themselves in rare alliance in condemning the pair's involvement. Eveleigh had not been an All Black since 1977 and Denholm never was and never would be, so the fuss soon died down and the union, perhaps realising it was in an invidious position, took no action.

The tour was a hugely enjoyable one, many players' wives being there adding to the enjoyment factor, and although it had a serious purpose – men such as Lochore and most of the players he had could not take rugby matches in South Africa with anything but the utmost seriousness – it lacked the nationalistic intensity of an All Black or Lions tour. The country was there to be enjoyed, the rugby was there to be enjoyed and if the matches were won, so much the better. Six out of the eight games were won, the losses being the last two Saturday matches, to Transvaal and the hosts, Northern Transvaal.

The members of the International XV, as it was known, wondered and marvelled at the contrasts that were South Africa and could fully understand the magnetism of the country to earlier generations and to generations to come. It wasn't just rugby, as Andy Haden eloquently explained in *Lock, Stock 'n Barrel*, talking about a visit to a game park: "This is South Africa as it was, as we all wish it could be . . . this Africa can so easily get into the blood. It creates a hunger to return, a hunger satisfied only by once again experiencing its enchantment."

` Haden also looked into the soul and psyche of South African rugby players, artfully using the expression, "bitter end", that had applied to the Afrikaner guerrillas in the Boer War, the "bitter enders" who waged war for 18 months after the British had captured the Boer capitals and annexed the republics of Transvaal and Orange Free State. "As tough and uncompromising as their heritage," Haden wrote, "obstinate to the bitter end and don't expect them to be any different in bowing to world opinion."

Though Lochore had no intentions of a return to active rugby participation at the national level, the tour partially prepared him for when that time came. The 1979 trip to South Africa had given him an insight so that the gap when he did return was not as great as it otherwise would have been. Helping close the gap had been players such as Haden, Oliver, Dalton, Knight and Donaldson who were experienced All Blacks and would build on that experience, in some cases, for several years.

Dalton recalled later that he developed a deep respect for Lochore as a coach on the tour. "This was my first experience with 'BJ' and was one of the reasons why I was so keen to tour with him again," Dalton wrote in *The Geriatrics*. "That had to be one of the greatest tests any coach faced for he had to bring together so many players, some of whom didn't speak English, from so many countries. Against all of those handicaps he came up with a fairly good side which in the circumstances performed better than could reasonably have been expected."

Lochore also provided some unbidden hilarity for the players. A stickler for discipline and correct behaviour from his players, Lochore was one day making a point about the need to respect property, especially in South Africa which had unhappy memories of the Lions "wreckers" of previous years. Lochore, Dalton recalled, chose to emphasise his point by thumping a table on which a large forward was reclining. The glass top of the table could not stand the combined force of a burly forward and the hand of a former forward and it shattered. Lochore's horrified expression, evidently, was a sight to behold.

The return to coaching when it came was neither sought by Lochore nor seen as inevitable by him, which was not the view of a lot of rugby people around the country who knew, suspected or just plain hoped that a man who had served his country so well as a player would return to serve it as a selector or as a coach.

The call when it came was after he had established Wairarapa-Bush in the first division. In the way these things can happen in rugby, first there was talk and a few tentative suggestions and, finally, a direct request: We'd like you to stand. Among Lochore's staunchest advocates on the New Zealand union was his old coach of the 1970 tour of South Africa, Ivan Vodanovich.

"That was around the end of the 1982 season and although I hadn't decided to finish as coach of Wairarapa-Bush, I knew it was a good time to relinquish it. I'm a firm believer that a coach shouldn't be there for longer than three years."

Lochore had reservations after he'd put down the phone to Vodanovich and other callers. He'd never had any ambition in rugby other than to be an All Black. Everything else had happened by accident or through a seeming inability to say no when asked to help. Nothing occurs of or by itself and everything hinges on some other occurrence. So it was with Lochore. He agreed to coach Masterton when he was still playing so he wouldn't have to make the eighty kilometre round trip later. His coaching of Masterton led him, in time, to the coaching of Wairarapa-Bush which, that task performed, led directly to the calls for him to take the next step, to the national panel.

This was where South Africa loomed again. "I guess people in 1982 were even then looking toward the South African tour of 1985 and saw me as someone having experience of playing there and knowing what was required to win a series there. The 1979 World tour was obviously a factor too because I had a more recent knowledge. I don't think this was intended as any disrespect to the coach at the time, Bryce Rope, and it certainly wasn't any disrespect on my part or intended as any criticism of him. What it came down to was that some people saw me as being suitable for the job as selector and perhaps they had an eye on the South African tour. No-one, of course, ever spelt that out and they wouldn't."

It's not that Lochore can't say no. He can. "I have no trouble saying no to things I don't think are worthwhile or wise. I suffer fools in silence and I know I can walk away when needed. But I guess I do have trouble saying no to things I believe in, especially when it comes to helping people or helping New Zealand."

Lochore's last New Zealand union role had been when he returned from "retirement" for the second test against the 1971 Lions.

Now he was back again, this time as a member of the national selection panel with convenor and coach Bryce Rope and Tiny Hill, the former All Black lock. It was a happy working relationship on the panel. Though Lochore had known Rope only slightly, they immediately got on well together. Lochore knew Hill better, though their careers had never previously crossed. As men who knew the bottom of an All Black ruck, they were of like minds.

All Black rugby in the early eighties went through what might be best described as a curious phase – the image suffered as a result of the South African tour of 1981, a tour in which Lochore played no part, and though the 1982 Australian tour went some way toward restoring the rugby-only image, there was still hovering in the background the prospect of the 1985 tour of South Africa. This was looked forward to by players and was the reason many extended their careers, but it was looked forward to with trepidation by some New Zealanders and revulsion by others.

The national feeling rubbed off on the players, Lochore observed. Though they were proud of being All Blacks, they were not so proud that they wanted to wear All Black jumpers in public and thus be identified. "The players suffered from the aftermath of 1981, they were conscious of it all the time. They suffered a great deal. Our job was to make them proud, make them proud to be All Blacks and proud to be representing New Zealand. But it wasn't easy in those days and I don't think it was something that really happened until 1987."

There were purely rugby concerns too. There was a suspicion by a great many people that the All Blacks more or less coached themselves and that, as a result, there was a lack of unified direction even though in 1983 they beat the British Isles four-nil in the tests. The sporting cachet of being an All Black also seemed to have lost some of its attraction when, later that year, several players made themselves unavailable for the tour of England and Scotland.

New Zealand trial, 1969. Meads 37, Lochore 19.

161

Sid Going hoists, v Wales, Lancaster Park, 1969.

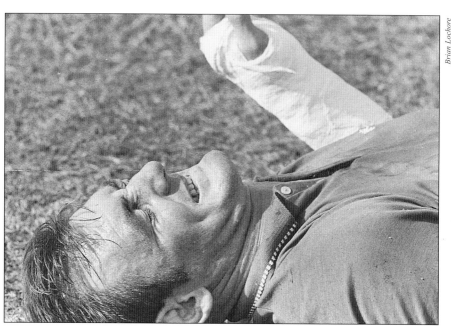

Horizontal agonising, South Africa, 1970.

Vertical agonising, East London, South Africa, 1970 – Lochore-Vodanovich, Wyllie-Muller, Kember-Williams.

Relief, a broken nose and an autograph. The Gazelles beaten 29-25, Potchefstroom, 1970.

Overleaf: Embracing Frik du Preez with affection. Northern Transvaal, 1970. (Brian Lochore)

Out of Africa . . . with Joanne, Pam, Sandra and David.

Comeback and farewell . . . the last hurrah. 1971, Athletic Park, meeting the Governor-General, Lord Porritt.

John Selkirk

Lochore at training before the first Rugby World Cup match, 1987.

John Selkirk

All Blacks selectors Hart, Wylie, Lochore at Eden Park to pick a team to go to Japan.

The dogs take us for a walk.

Though Lochore was a national selector, he was nothing more than an intensely interested observer. He contributed to the selections – the introduction of Jock Hobbs and Warwick Taylor for the Lions series, for example – but had no coaching role and did not even attend All Black training sessions. The All Blacks were Rope's and the Colts were Hill's and Lochore was satisfied with that situation. He had no complaints. Neither then nor now was he critical of Rope's coaching of the All Blacks, though he was aware that some players had more influence than perhaps they should have.

Lochore did not believe then, or now, that coaches should move in cold, least of all with such a flagbearing team as the All Blacks. "Whoever takes over the All Blacks should have been coaching immediately prior to that. It's not ideal for someone to go in cold. They could spend three or four years on the panel first coaching other teams and observing, and then take over. You can select till you're 60, but you can't coach till then. It's a big responsibility."

Lochore believes so much in the paramountcy of the coach that he advocates the coach being able to nominate his fellow selectors, a state in New Zealand rugby that has almost been reached.

Lochore's job in 1983, primarily, was to look, listen and learn, to gather as much information as possible about players for both the short- and long-term futures. "Tiny and I didn't go to trainings and, in some cases, I didn't even know some of the All Blacks. An indication of our role in 1983 is that we were just insets in the team photos."

Some of the players for the future had to be called on earlier than expected when so many withdrew from the tour of England and Scotland. One of the selection panel's greatest difficulties for that tour was deciding who would be captain. Andy Dalton, a masterful leader who had captained the All Blacks against the Lions, was unavailable and there was no obvious replacement.

They eventually settled on wing Stu Wilson because he was

so experienced and part of that experience had been tours of Britain in successive years, 1978-79-80. The selectors were conscious that wing was not the best position from which to captain a side and that Wilson, in ideal circumstances, was more of a lieutenant than a captain, a charming and lively individual and not ideally suited to the responsibility of captain. He was one of the boys rather than a leader of men. But the experience outweighed all.

"It was a touring side and we needed someone who understood touring and who had had experience in that part of the world and that was the basis on which Wilson was chosen," Lochore said. "If the selection had been for tests in New Zealand, Wilson would probably not have been chosen. On-field captaincy is not so much of a burden, but the job of a touring captain is much more onerous. We had the option of giving the captaincy to someone of experience or taking a punt on someone totally out of the blue."

And, contrary to widespread belief, All Black selectors have no more hindsight than anyone else. In that team that drew with Scotland and lost to England were two future All Black captains of distinction, Jock Hobbs and David Kirk. It's easy in later years to point out such facts.

By the following year, 1984, the unavailable became available again because of the prospect of South Africa and Lochore found himself more actively involved in selecting and, for the first time, coaching nationally.

While the All Blacks played France at home and toured Australia, Lochore's prime responsibility was the Colts, the national under-21 side that in many ways is a proving ground for the All Blacks. Selecting Colts sides was more difficult, or more haphazard, than it is now. Then, selectors had to rely on nominations from provincial unions and on pedigree, aside from those few players they had seen in provincial sides. If a nominated player had played for island age teams or the national secondary schools side, he would have a greater chance of getting into the Colts than those who had not, irrespective of current form. Now, prospective Colts are seen in more provincial matches and are taken to the Police College at Porirua for several days of training and assessments and it's much more assured that the selectors will net the players they need.

Selecting any team will never be an exact science and selecting Colts teams is even less likely to be. Some players, especially Polynesians, mature earlier and therefore stand out in the late teen years; others may not fully develop as rugby players until they are past the age when they can be Colts. There's also a large fallout from Colts teams – only a small percentage take the logically progressive step and become All Blacks. That may partly be because players lose interest or find other interests, but another factor is that the later-maturing players catch up.

One of Lochore's early lessons with the Colts was one he least expected. It was a dietary lesson. "They ate a hell of a lot," he recalled, "and the more the tour went on, the worse they played. I couldn't figure it out. Our training was OK, I reckon I had the best players I could have had, and I hadn't forgotten that much about coaching. Then I realised that they were eating too much and too much of the wrong food and it affected their fitness. It was something that had not been looked at with Colts teams before."

Lochore does not have especially happy memories of his return to coaching. "It was a new challenge but I didn't enjoy the results and we had not a particularly pleasant few days in Australia. We stayed in a motel that could only be described as adequate. One of the players came to me and complained that they had three to a room, one of them on a camp stretcher between the two beds. This wasn't on and it took a bit of intensive debating with the Australians to get it fixed. Apparently their Colts had been put in army quarters or something in New Zealand the year before and this was their way of paying us back.

"We weren't asking for flash, five-star hotels but we did

expect better than that. It didn't start the Australian visit off on a very good note and it didn't get any better."

Lochore's Colts played Australia under-21 in the curtain-raiser to the All Blacks' first test against Australia at the Sydney Cricket Ground. Both matches were lost, the Colts 10-12 and the All Blacks 9-16. It was not a great day for New Zealand rugby.

It was made worse for the Colts because instead of sharing the after-match function with the test teams, they were stuck away in a room of their own and given what Lochore described as a pie and a bottle of fizzy drink. "The Colts were very much an after-thought, very much an appendage. They were looking forward to mixing with the All Blacks and the Wallabies after the game and it would have been part of the learning experience for them, but they were denied that."

It was a Colts team that would have a significant bearing on the future of New Zealand rugby. Lochore was the coach, of course, and the manager was Richie Guy, soon to be the All Black manager and later to be the chairman of the New Zealand union during its period of most turbulent change.

Among the players were future All Blacks Mark Finlay, Bernie McCahill, Frano Botica, Paul Henderson, Chris Tregaskis, Ron Williams and the most capped test player of them all, Sean Fitzpatrick.

And in an early indication of things to come, Fitzpatrick was the Colts captain. "I needed someone with the mana to lead and off the field was as important as on the field," Lochore said. "Sean was someone they all respected both as a player and as a leader. At that level, it's a bit difficult to judge what they're like tactically on the field but in all respects Sean was a most successful captain and it led to me recommending to Bryce and to future selection panels that if they were looking for a captain, Fitzpatrick could do the job more than adequately. I considered then that he was potentially a future All Black captain."

It established Lochore as a judge of players and a prophet of no mean ability. Fitzpatrick became All Black captain under coach Laurie Mains in 1992 and was to keep the job without a break for the next five seasons.

7
A TIME OF DISRUPTION

The visitors to Brian and Pam Lochore's home in the Wairarapa have been many and varied. To many of the visitors, it has been a place of pilgrimage, a meeting of rugby minds and shared reminiscences of games and times past. Some have gone there on missions, seeking this or that from Lochore, some have gone for a chat and others have gone just to say "Hi" to a great man of rugby.

Not many could have gone there to talk international politics. One did. Sam Ramsamy was a name well-known to New Zealanders through the seventies and eighties as the country went through the agonies of the debate about playing sport with, and particularly rugby against, South Africa. He is a South African who, unable to live under apartheid, moved to London where he became a focal point for the international campaign against the white, Afrikaner regime. He became a key member of an organisation called the South African Non-Racial Olympic Committee (Sanroc), a sort of South African sports umbrella body in exile, living for the day apartheid was dismantled. He achieved his goals beyond what even he may have imagined and now is an influential man in South African sport and a member of the International Olympic Committee.

Ramsamy, in the early eighties when the South African debate was always an issue, visited New Zealand in his continuing endeavours to try to dissuade any contact with a country whose government he saw as detestable. A friend of Lochore's in Masterton was passionately opposed to contact with South Africa and it was because of his suggestion that Ramsamy ended up at the Lochore home for lunch.

"This chap in Masterton phoned me one day and said that Ramsamy would be in Masterton and suggested I should meet him," Lochore recalled. "I didn't hesitate. 'Bring him out,' I told him, and he did. He was with us for about an hour and a half, had lunch with us, and we had a very amicable discussion. He made his points politely and I listened and I made my points politely and listened.

"The thing that struck me though was that he was talking about a South Africa that he had known but knew no more. He was talking about things that happened in South Africa when, quite clearly, they did not happen. I had more recent experience of South Africa than he did and I was surprised to learn that he was sadly misinformed. During the whole debate over the years, New Zealanders found this difficult to understand. Sure, apartheid was still in place and the whites were running the country, but there was change and I had seen it. Sam Ramsamy, a man who had spoken to the United Nations about South Africa and who talked to politicians all over the world, had not seen the gradual changes and he talked about a South Africa that had been. He was out of date."

Lochore and Ramsamy agreed to differ over means rather than the end. "We both wanted to do the same thing, we both wanted the same result, we just differed on how to achieve that result. I am not a racist and he knew I was not a racist. I was trying to do my bit against apartheid by maintaining contact and by insisting that sport breaks down barriers; he was doing his bit in quite the opposite way, through isolation."

As Lochore's coaching career developed, so did his unwilling and unwanted immersion in the South African issue, the Great Debate of New Zealand life.

By the end of 1984, talk in rugby centred on the South African tour planned for 1985, the talk almost evenly and neatly divided into the purely rugby aspects – Who would go? Could they at last win a series in South Africa? – and the political – Should they go? Would they go?

Some newspapers had suggested that Lochore would be the coach, that this after all was why he had been brought onto the national panel two years before. It was evident that this was the way a majority of the 19 members of the New Zealand Rugby Football Union council were thinking too and as their December meeting approached, the meeting that would appoint the manager for the tour and the selectors for the following year, speculation increased.

"I was aware of the rumblings," Lochore recalled, "but I didn't actively lobby for or seek the coach's job. I had made myself available as I had been asked to do, but that was as far as it went. My attitude was no different to what it had been. It was a challenge I was prepared for but if I hadn't been elected coach, it wouldn't have been the end of the world and I would have been happy to be just a member of the panel again."

When the council voted and Lochore was named selection convenor, and therefore coach, it was not a surprise to the country as a whole. This was, after all, people supposed, part of the grand plan all along. It was bad luck for Bryce Rope, people thought, but whatever Rope's qualities, he did not have the standing and reputation of Lochore, especially for such a demanding time and tour that was now on the horizon.

"Bryce was a gentleman," Lochore said. "He accepted the decision like a gentleman. There were never any cross words or anything like that, there was no tension when we first met. It was business as usual with just a rearrangement of roles. We functioned as smoothly with me as convenor as we had with Bryce in the chair."

Lochore's thoughts and energies were directed almost entirely toward New Zealand rugby's most challenging and demanding tour. It never occurred to him that it might not go ahead and New Zealand's top fifty or sixty players vying for places on the tour of tours were of a like mind. Many of the players had been at the top level since the mid to late seventies and, clearly, had continued so they could bow out on the highest note of all: a series win in South Africa. As rugby players, it was their ultimate goal.

Only the high-level rugby player can really understand the attraction of a tour of South Africa. Only he can appreciate the deep-seated urge to try to conquer there for the first time. Unlike most New Zealanders, the top rugby players are used to winning in the international arena. For many tests, the need to win is not enough for the All Blacks. They need to win with style or by a large points margin to gain satisfaction from a match. They have won so often they feel the need to do more than just win and they know the public of New Zealand demands it as well. Public expectations of the All Blacks are higher than for any other national sports team or individual. The public wants and hopes others will win, it demands that the All Blacks do so. South Africa at the beginning of 1985 was the last challenge for the All Blacks. The Springboks had then been beaten in series in New Zealand on three occasions, but five times the All Blacks had gone to the land of their nemesis and failed each time. It sticks in the craw.

As the early months of 1985 came and went and the tour came nearer, rugby expectations rose in direct proportion to the volume of the wider opposition to the tour. The genuinely concerned, the cynics and the ill-informed advanced all manner of accusations against rugby in general and All Blacks in particular and offered a variety of reasons why they thought the All Blacks were, in their words, prepared to flout international opinion. There was talk of sackfuls of krugerrands and lavish hospitality in South Africa but the more thoughtful of the tour opponents knew well that the All Blacks' motivation was not for material reward but for the simple joy of winning something that had not been won before or, failing that, at least to try. The fact it was such a simple, basic aim made it even harder for opponents to understand. Some did not want to understand.

Before South Africa, Lochore had to choose and coach teams to play England and Australia, matches which turned out to be eminently forgettable. South Africa dominated all and though Lochore and his captain, Andy Dalton, insisted and insisted again that the focus must be on the opponents of today, not of tomorrow, it was evident and inevitable that matches against the Springboks had a permanent, immovable place in players' minds. It was also extremely trying and difficult, and in some cases upsetting, for players to try to concentrate on their matches against England or Australia against an unending barrage of abuse from people protesting against the tour. This, of course, was precisely what the protesters intended.

"It was not a very nice position to be in," Lochore recalled with remarkable understatement. "There were difficulties on all sorts of fronts. The continuing arguments and debates were wearying and the All Blacks were hurt by some of the things said about them. It's not very nice being in a position when you're trying to help race relations, you're trying in your way to break down apartheid, and you're being attacked all the time.

"Preparation was very difficult. We were all feeling the heat of the abuse and the isolation enforced by security. These guys just wanted to be All Blacks. They didn't want to change the world, though they would have loved South Africa to be a country that was acceptable to the rest of the world. They didn't want anything to do with politics or other issues.

"In Christchurch [for the first test against England] there were bomb scares in the middle of the night, people were chanting outside the hotel all night so that we had to rearrange the rooms so the guys who were playing were on the inside and sheltered as best they could be against the interference.

"There was a constant police presence and they did a great job in very difficult circumstances. They were as unobtrusive as they could be at the same time as trying to do their job. They weren't there to protect us, they were there to preserve the peace. They would advise us about how to avoid confrontation and further controversy and it was very difficult trying to think of rugby in that atmosphere.

"I remember after training one day at Rugby Park there were no buses and we had to get taxis back to the hotel. While we waited for the taxis, we just had to stand there in the face of unrelenting abuse. The language was appalling, especially from the women. We couldn't do anything, say anything, just stand there and let it wash over us."

The players then and later spoke in their private moments about how the demonstrations affected them, how it felt to be an All Black training to play for your country and someone was standing near you shouting, over and over again, your name and not to go.

"John Ashworth, don't go!" The cry would go up not once, not twice, but innumerable times. "Andy Dalton, don't go!" screamed in your face, over and over again.

Lochore felt it himself, but felt more for his players. "You're never going to play well if you know a percentage of your country is against you," he said. "The guys were not proud of their All Black blazers, they didn't want to wear anything that identified them as All Blacks. They were haunted and hunted men in their own country.

It was not pleasant, enduring such hatred at home. We knew that once we got away that wouldn't be a problem, that on tour a team becomes an entity in itself and that we would be stronger. But first we had to get away."

Getting away, as it turned out, was the most difficult bit. Before then, there was England and Australia. Lochore had introduced three players new to test rugby for the first test in Christchurch – the Taranaki fullback, Kieran Crowley, who proved to be the saviour; David Kirk, who had toured England and Scotland in 1983 and Australia in 1984; and the Wellington lock Murray Pierce, who had toured Australia the year before.

England were not a strong side, short on experience and short, so it seemed from their lead-up games, on ideas. But they nearly beat New Zealand in Christchurch and were prevented from doing so only by Crowley kicking six penalty goals. The All Blacks' mediocre performance, attributed to "first test blues" that sometimes seem to afflict New Zealand teams, was in truth more attributable to the less than ideal preparation they had had. Mentally, the All Blacks were far from ready for a test match.

It was better the following week in Wellington, mainly because the All Blacks were able to rise above their peripheral problems and correct some of the faults of Christchurch. They played more like an All Black team is expected to play and won 42-15.

Three weeks later came the Australian test at Eden Park and this was almost a reversion to the form of Christchurch. It was a lacklustre game, attributable to each side's familiarity of the other's ploys but also not helped as a spectacle by refereeing that was strong on the laws but short on the spirit. The test was won by a tap penalty move engineered by Andy Dalton and executed to perfection by Craig Green.

No-one knew it at the time, but the test marked the end of the international careers of Dalton, John Ashworth, Steve Pokere and Murray Mexted. Such distinguished careers needed a more fitting finale.

In the background always was South Africa and Lochore, like everyone else, followed every move, sometimes with cynicism, sometimes with wonder, sometimes with disgust, sometimes with delight, always with intense interest.

The rugby union had twice affirmed its intention to carry on with the tour in the face of a unanimous resolution from Parliament and a directive from the Prime Minister that his deputy conceded had no backing in law. The union took heart from the view of Parliament which was that "the decision whether to tour or not is one for the Rugby Union alone and accepts that the Government must always preserve the right of all New Zealanders to act without intimidation provided their actions are within the law."

Between the England and Australian tests in June 1985, a greater threat than even Parliament was stirring, at first regarded as a token effort to stop the tour but as it carried on it became apparent it was a very serious threat indeed. It was the legal action by two Aucklanders with rugby affiliations, Patrick Finnigan and Phillip Recordon, that the tour was against the union's constitutional objectives of promoting, controlling and fostering rugby.

Lochore and his fellow selectors, trying to decide on the 30 players they would take to South Africa, watched from afar with an interest that began as passing and rapidly became intense. The contention was initially thrown out of court but it went to the Appeal Court and it decided Finnigan and Recordon could indeed proceed against the rugby union. "The appellants cannot be dismissed as mere busybodies, cranks or mischief makers," the Appeal Court president, Sir Robin Cooke, said. That woke New Zealanders – and Lochore and the All Blacks – up to the dawning fact that the threat was very real indeed.

The team, meanwhile, was chosen. Lochore had made it very clear he wanted only an All Black team capable of beating the Springboks. He did not want time-servers, he did not want players for whom the attainment of All Black status was a goal in itself. He, better than the players, knew how terribly difficult it was to win a series in South Africa.

Rugby union chairman Ces Blazey announced the team on the Wednesday after the Australian test. It was, by consensus, a selection that reflected the current strengths of New Zealand rugby. There were no surprise omissions, one or two surprise inclusions (most notably the Taranaki wing, Bryce Robins), and marked a comeback for the Taranaki halfback, Dave Loveridge, who had been out for a year because of a knee injury that would have finished lesser careers.

Most of the players had been involved in the matches against England and Australia and had had in Auckland a taste of the legal problems to come. The rugby union's lawyers had briefed the team on the background to the unusual court action taking place and outlined what possible outcomes there could be. It was the first realisation by the players that the court action was so serious that it could indeed stop the tour.

Five days after the team had been named, the legal action was back in the High Court. It was now a matter of the utmost immediacy to Lochore and the players.

Lochore was clear about his course of action. If the action failed, the tour would go ahead and he would do what he was elected to do. If it succeeded, or if there was some sort of settlement, he would do what the rugby union or the government (not necessarily in that order) said he must do.

"Toward the end of the trial I was asked by the union's lawyers if I'd take the stand," Lochore said. "I said I would if they thought it would help. I must say I agreed reluctantly. The intention was for me to talk about how I thought the tour would help break down attitudes in South Africa and would help rugby among the blacks and the Coloureds. I was to talk about my experiences there in 1970 and 1979 and how the situation in South Africa was not exactly as it was painted in New Zealand.

"I had never been in court before in my life. I had my own guided tour, the lawyers showed me where the witness box was and where the bench was. There was no-one there at the time. We went off to lunch, expecting to go back in the afternoon. During lunch, we got a call from the plaintiff's lawyers suggesting that because of the lack of time my evidence should be given by affidavit instead and the union's lawyers agreed."

It was a cunning ploy.

Lochore thought then, and still thinks now, that such a course of action weakened the union's case considerably. Lochore recalled how he sat in the public gallery of the court in

183

the afternoon and listened to a pack of lies about South Africa. "I didn't think the NZRFU case had been put well at all and from that point I think I knew what the outcome would be."

Finnigan and Recordon, through their QC, Ted Thomas, had applied for an interim injunction to stop the All Blacks from leaving. Mr Justice Casey heard the arguments and retired to consider his verdict.

Lochore headed back home. Justice Casey broke the suspense on a Saturday afternoon, at a time when club rugby was being played throughout the country, when some of those most affected were either playing or watching. They heard the news in various ways. Some on the radio. Some told by friends. Some by phone. Some were prepared for it, some were not. Some understood, some did not. All were devastated. Numbed. Justice Casey had donned a metaphorical black cap for them all.

He said in his oral judgment that it had long been recognised that the court had jurisdiction to make orders preserving the status quo until the dispute between the parties had been disposed of by further hearings. He emphasised that the granting or refusal of an injunction was not the final ruling on the claim, nor was it any indication of how the court might eventually rule.

They were learned, legal words. They were cold comfort. The tour was off.

"I was at home and I first heard the news on the radio," Lochore recalled. "I was numb. When you work for something and it's taken away from you, you're left numb. It's as if a part of you has been taken away, cut off.

"The phone rang more or less constantly for two weeks. The players were shattered, their rugby life in tatters. They'd been thinking of little else for years. Every time you went for a run, you'd run a wee bit harder and a wee bit longer because you'd think of South Africa. It was devastating for them. They needed to talk.

"I did my best to console them, but what do you say? What

do you say to guys like Gary Knight and John Ashworth? There's no challenges left for them. They knew that. The ends of their careers had been taken away from them."

The calls were not just from players. There were calls from reporters, some known to Lochore, most of them not. Some were polite and rang at respectable hours, many were not and did not. Some were abrasive and rude, giving their views rather than eliciting information, denying the ethics of their job to make their own valueless points.

"I had no trouble with the reporters I knew and who knew me. But it was international news and I was dealing with reporters who didn't know me and some who seemed to know little about rugby or New Zealand. That was probably the hardest part of the whole time. I grew up rather quickly."

It wasn't long before the calls came about touring anyway, about an alternative tour, not as All Blacks representing the New Zealand union, but as individuals. They were tentative at first, then more detailed.

Lochore was ambivalent. An official, authorised tour was one thing, a rebel tour quite another, especially for Lochore whose loyalty was to his players but also to the body that appointed him, the rugby union. "I didn't discourage the talk at that stage," he recalled, "but I certainly counselled the players on the need for something of substance. If they were going to do this sort of thing, they had to think it through, think of the consequences not just for themselves, but also for their families, and also whether what they were thinking of doing was good for rugby."

Lochore, after talking at length on the phone with Dalton, told the players to cool it, to wait so any decision was made coldly and clinically and not in the heat of the moment.

Prime Minister David Lange unwittingly had sown in some of the players' minds the idea of the rebel tour because he'd said, after the injunction had been granted and when he was asked about individual rights, that there was nothing to prevent the All

Blacks going to South Africa as individuals. What the court forbade was a New Zealand Rugby Football Union tour.

The whole party that would have toured was summoned to Wellington early the following week to hear what the union had to say. It had little to say, mainly because lawyers pointed out to the players that under the terms of the injunction, South Africa could not be discussed with New Zealand union councillors. Lochore, as a servant of the union, was prevented from joining his players in the meeting at which they decided – at the union's suggestion – they would go to Argentina instead.

But even this was denied them. The players returned home and a day later, on the Thursday, the union said Argentina was unable to host a tour at such short notice. Those players who had been arguing all along to go to South Africa anyway regained the ascendancy.

They were helped by Blazey saying the union had cancelled all plans to attempt a South African tour, that the High Court case would not be pursued but leave would be sought to go to the Privy Council in London over the Appeal Court's initial decision to allow the case to proceed. That avenue was eventually denied the union.

A private tour of South Africa was back on the top of the agenda and players agreed to meet in Auckland early the following week. Some were in Auckland by the Sunday, eight days after the injunction had been granted. Some South Island players, in the grandest of cloak and dagger tradition, drove to Picton in what Lochore remembered as a clapped-out van and on the interisland ferry wore sunglasses, balaclavas and over-sized coats in an effort to appear incognito. Secrecy in mounting the tour was paramount. But few All Blacks can appear in public in New Zealand without being recognised. A ferry worker recognised the balaclava'd Wayne Smith and said to him, "Hi Smithy, what's going on? Half the Canterbury team are on board!"

Plans for the tour had rapidly gone ahead and, despite the

best efforts of all involved to keep it quiet, speculation in the news media was intense, some of it close to what was going on but some wide of the mark. Dave Loveridge's wife, Janine, stayed at her parents' home in Auckland. Neighbours called in for a visit and when they saw her sitting there they exclaimed, "So it's all true! You're going!"

Nothing was ever straightforward, as Lochore and the others discovered. The same weekend the touring party was surreptitiously preparing to go, increased rioting in black townships mainly around Johannesburg and east of Cape Town prompted South Africa to declare a state of emergency. On the Sunday, 113 people had been arrested. The state of emergency, the first since the Sharpeville massacre in 1960, allowed the government to impose curfews, censor the press and detain people indefinitely without a warrant.

Reading and hearing of this, some of the players started to have second thoughts and Lochore, still at home but constantly on the phone, urged caution. The next day, after repeated calls to South Africa, the players learned the rioting was localised and the danger was not as real as first feared.

"We did not want to act irresponsibly or appear to be acting irresponsibly, but we were prepared to go even if it was in breach of the court order," Lochore said. "We were, in our view, ordinary citizens and we were going to South Africa as ordinary citizens. We were all individual New Zealanders.

"We also felt that we were doing something that probably the majority of New Zealanders wished us to do, and maybe the New Zealand union as well. Certainly some of the councillors knew what was going on, though they could play no role and had to deny they knew.

"I knew I was jeopardising my role as chairman of selectors but, for the players' sake, I was prepared to give that up. They were being denied what was rightfully theirs and I felt deeply for them. They were hurt. So I was helping the players, but at the same time not necessarily helping myself."

Another day, another decision. On the Tuesday, ten days after the injunction, came the death knell. Ted Thomas, counsel for Finnigan and Recordon, telexed the rugby union's lawyers and said that any breach of the court order would be met with proceedings for contempt. "Our instructions are to act promptly against any subterfuge or connivance designed to circumvent the injunction," he said. It was also argued that specifically forbidden from going were "servants and agents of the union" and into that category were Lochore, captain Andy Dalton and lock Andy Haden, who, in one of the great rugby ironies, had recently been appointed marketing consultant to the union.

About 16 or 17 of the players met in Auckland that afternoon and discussed the prospect of touring without the man who had chosen them and would coach them, without their captain and without their principal lock who had also been one of the main organisers. They voted against going.

"There didn't seem to be any point to it anymore," Loveridge recalled. "I didn't want to go there in such circumstances – and we thought there might be increased reaction in New Zealand against us – and go there and not have a show of achieving what we wanted, to beat South Africa."

Lochore was told of the decision about an hour before he was due to leave home for the airport. "It had to be all or nothing," he said. "In the end, we took the responsible attitude. We could not go in such circumstances. Uppermost in our minds was the state of emergency in South Africa, even though things by then seemed to have quietened down. New Zealanders wouldn't have accepted us being there where people could be shot. We couldn't guarantee the safety of the players."

Staying in touch with Ces Blazey and the rugby union secretary, Barry Usmar, added to the Lochore phone bill as he constantly reminded them of how the players suffered. Both men were sympathetic and it was through their efforts that Argentine officials were persuaded to change their mind and say that yes, after all, the All Blacks could go there.

To get away from it all, and especially to get away from telephones, Brian and Pam Lochore and Andy and Pip Dalton went to Turangi for a few days. They did not remain undetected for long. They went to play golf, found it was ladies' day and they were immediately recognised by the good women golfers of Turangi. "What are you lot doing here?" they chorused. The unwitting hosts were delighted with their guests and they got together for a long and enjoyable lunch.

The Argentine tour was set for October and there was never any doubt in Lochore's mind, or in Blazey's, that though the domestic season had to be played out – including the gripping Ranfurly Shield match when Auckland took the shield from Canterbury – the players chosen for South Africa would also be going to Argentina. That was the least they deserved. In the event, three of those originally chosen, captain Dalton, prop John Ashworth and midfield back Bill Osborne, made themselves unavailable and were replaced by Bruce Hemara of Manawatu, Brian McGrattan of Wellington and Kurt Sherlock of Auckland. Jock Hobbs, who'd made his debut two years before against the Lions and whose legal training had thrust him into the role as wise counsel to the players through the anxieties of 1985, took over from Dalton as captain.

The Argentine tour, as enjoyable as it was in a country that is refreshingly different from what touring rugby players are used to, was compensation. That was all. It was never, and could never have been, the real thing. The players had geared themselves, physically and mentally, for South Africa. They got Argentina instead. Lochore's preparations had been for South Africa. Argentina was not the same. There was also a tinge of sadness for Lochore that not all the players he had chosen for South Africa could also go to Argentina. He felt for the three who didn't go, but most especially felt for Dalton, whose commitment to winning in South Africa had been total.

"Though it wasn't what we really wanted, Argentina was still a serious rugby tour where test matches had to be won," Lochore said. "People at home might have seen it as a bit of a Cook's tour but I can assure you it wasn't that. The results of the tests [the first won, the second drawn] were proof of that. The Pumas were as strong then as they've ever been and I'd think were at least the equal of the European teams, perhaps better than some. It was a demanding tour, but fun all the same, though it was never what it was intended to be. I think South Africa was in the backs of our minds all the time."

8
BABY-SITTER

B rian Lochore in 1986 was in his second year as All Black coach and, in the philosophy that guided him then and to which he still adheres, it should have been the year of consolidation. In the Lochore coaching manual, the first year is the year of getting organised; the second year is for building on the foundation and the third year should be the year of culmination, the time when everything comes together. At the end of it, the coach should be able to walk away, satisfied with a job well done.

Things don't always go according to plan, as Parkinson might have said. It might have even been one of Murphy's laws. Whoever and whatever, it became one of Lochore's lessons of life along the way.

The year, in a rugby sense, began as the previous one had ended. South Africa. The primeval desire, the need, to beat the Springboks on their own damned veld, high and low, was to be as disruptive to Lochore's plans in 1986 as it had been in 1985.

The year began in different places for different people. For some, it began in Hong Kong. Or, to be more accurate, the rugby year of 1986 began for some in the calendar year of 1985 in Hong Kong. It was at a small gathering of New Zealand and South African rugby people whose aim was to resurrect in some form the abandoned tour of South Africa. Among the New Zealanders were two All Blacks, Andy Dalton and Andy Haden, captain and first lieutenant of The Team That Didn't Go, and a former All Black captain of considerable distinction, Ian Kirkpatrick. Among the South Africans were one of the most powerful men in South Africa, Louis Luyt, and Robert Denton, the man who six years before had hauled Lochore out of his rugby hibernation and set him, unwittingly, on his coaching path. Denton now was manager of Ellis Park, headquarters of Transvaal, the province that was home base for Luyt's expanding empire. Also at the meeting was an Auckland businessman, Winston McDonald, who always seemed to be there or thereabouts when New Zealand-South Africa rugby contact was being discussed.

Lochore at home in the Wairarapa knew nothing of this meeting at the time. He was to learn of it later when Kirkpatrick, who began his illustrious career under Lochore's captaincy and who captained the All Blacks himself in 1972-73, reported to Lochore its purpose and its decisions. Kirkpatrick had been approached by Haden to manage the 1985 All Blacks under another name, later determined as the Cavaliers, on an unauthorised and then-secret tour of South Africa. Would Lochore, Kirkpatrick wanted to know, be the coach.

At the December meeting of the New Zealand Rugby Union, Lochore had been reappointed convenor of selectors. On the programme for 1986 was a quick visit by France including a single test, a three-test tour by Australia and, in October and November, a tour of France. More significantly, the International Rugby Board the previous year had agreed to introduce a World Cup and the first would be staged in New Zealand and Australia in 1987. Some rugby countries were dubious about the merits of a World Cup and Lochore too had his doubts, but he knew that if the All Blacks were to win it or at least perform as well as they were able, planning was paramount and could not wait till 1987.

Lochore did not hesitate when Kirkpatrick popped his question. Thanks for the offer, he said, but no thanks. "It was quite plain to me that I could not wear two hats in my position," Lochore recalled. "As much as I sympathised with what the players wanted to do, I had been appointed chairman of the New Zealand selectors and coach of the All Blacks and my responsibilities lay in New Zealand. I could not go on any unauthorised tour, whether to South Africa or anywhere else."

Kirkpatrick, perhaps one of the under-valued men of New Zealand rugby, immediately accepted Lochore's decision. He did not try to persuade him to change his mind, nor implore him to reconsider.

For the rest of the sad chapter of the Cavaliers in New Zealand rugby history, Lochore figured hardly at all. He had no role, nor even any information, about the planning of the tour, though he knew, of course, that it was going ahead, which was more than most of New Zealand knew.

Lochore's stature among the rest of the rugby world as a player had never been questioned, and certainly not after the 1967 tour. Now, his stature as a coach, even given the interrupted time at the top he had had, was becoming acknowledged.

The International Rugby Board in early 1986 celebrated its centenary and, to mark the occasion, two commemorative games were staged, one the British Isles versus The Rest in Cardiff, the other Overseas Unions versus the Five Nations. Lochore was asked by the IRB to look after the overseas teams, an honour indeed for one who still sometimes refers to himself as a Wairarapa farm boy. The British stage these sorts of occasions particularly well – the attention to detail, the "form" and the proper way of doing things, the formal dinners and the reminiscences of games won and lost, the memories of absent friends, as the cigars and the port are passed around. Nowhere is there greater acknowledgement than in the IRB, despite appearances sometimes, that rugby is the ultimate player's game, that the game is for the players and everything else is subordinate, and Lochore felt both comfortable and humble in such circumstances. He was especially honoured with his involvement with the game in Cardiff, which marked only the second official time the British Isles had played at home. The first had been against the Barbarians at Twickenham in 1977 to mark the Queen's silver jubilee.

For all the players' criticism, public and private, in the mid-eighties of the administration of the game and especially of the IRB and its gin-sipping image redolent of old Empire at the East India Club in St James's in London, the elite of rugby's elite played in the games. There had probably never been a finer collection of the world's great rugby-playing talent in one place at one time as there was in Cardiff and London in April 1986. Among them were several All Blacks – wing John Kirwan, second five-eighth Warwick Taylor, first five-eighth Wayne Smith, halfback Dave Loveridge, number eight Murray Mexted, flanker Mark Shaw, lock Andy Haden, prop Gary Knight and hooker Andy Dalton. To Dalton went the singular acknowledgement as captain of the Overseas Unions who beat the Five Nations at Twickenham 32-13. A French quartet invited, Serge Blanco, Patrick Esteve, Philippe Sella and Jean Condom, had a foot in both camps. They were with the Rest of the World to play the Lions then had to switch sides to play for the Five Nations. Their reluctant departure after Cardiff made it plain to Lochore which side they preferred to be with.

The All Blacks were not just there for the celebrations. They told Lochore in Britain that, with the exception of Kirwan, they were going on to South Africa to meet up with their thwarted teammates of the year before. "They did me the courtesy of telling me what they were doing and, although I couldn't join them, I understood why they were doing it," Lochore said.

Also at the celebrations were two veteran IRB members, retiring New Zealand chairman Ces Blazey and the patriarch of South African rugby, Danie Craven. It was during that week that Blazey accosted Craven and demanded to know what was going on. He too had heard the rumours. Craven denied any knowledge – a denial that was later proved to be false – and Blazey recalled years later, partly with anger and partly with amusement, that when he told Craven that such a tour as was then being mooted was unacceptable, Craven, whose English was fluent if sometimes guttural, turned to a colleague and said:

"What does 'unacceptable' mean?"

Lochore returned to New Zealand wondering what the consequences of the Cavaliers tour would be, not knowing then that he would have to choose an almost entirely new All Black team to play France and Australia. Only he and Tiny Hill of the national selection panel were in New Zealand. Colin Meads, the legendary Pinetree, had replaced Bryce Rope on the panel but had accepted Kirkpatrick's offer to go to South Africa as coach of the Cavaliers.

"Colin had phoned me and told me he'd been asked to go and that it was his intention to go," Lochore said. "He reasoned that for all the flak he was likely to get, he at least would be in South Africa watching 30 of New Zealand's top players.

"What he did was entirely his own decision and I told him it could only be his decision. I could say neither yes nor no to him, but I understood his position."

Meads was and is another example of how deeply the South African ties lie in New Zealand rugby minds. The depth of feeling is perhaps understood only by those who share it, rather than by those who merely observe it.

By the time France were in New Zealand on their flying visit, the Cavaliers – or most of them – were home from their 12-match tour, having lost the series to South Africa and also having lost, at an early stage, their captain, Andy Dalton, because of a broken jaw. In a playing sense, the tour was not a success. In a wider rugby sense, its achievements or otherwise were entirely in the minds of the beholders.

The New Zealand union, incensed by the tour and especially by the duplicitous role Craven and the South African union had played – a union New Zealand had in years past bent over backwards to help, often to its cost – had declared all the Cavaliers ineligible for the French test on the basis of a little-enforced residency rule. It then suspended them for one international, the first against Australia. It also demanded from them affidavits swearing they had not been paid on the tour,

195

affidavits that were duly forwarded to the union. The issue of whether they were paid became, after their return, a greater issue than the fact they went at all when they were not supposed to. Under the new chairmanship of Russ Thomas, it was one of the union's last big skirmishes on the battlefield of amateurism and its result was much the same as all the other skirmishes in the name of that vexed issue: inconclusive.

So Lochore and Hill, later rejoined by Meads who had been "reprimanded" by the union's council, were faced with what Lochore had suspected all along they would be faced with: choosing a new All Black team to play France. It wouldn't be entirely new. Kirwan and David Kirk of the 1985 All Blacks had not gone to South Africa so were available, but it was so new that among Lochore's first duties when they assembled in Christchurch was to introduce some players to one another.

"Boy, they were raw," Lochore recalled. "We assembled on a Wednesday and the first get-together really was a getting-to-know-you affair. The training on the Thursday was at the Burnham military camp and it was disastrous. They scrummaged badly, the lineout throwing was rough, but everyone was trying so hard, I think probably too hard. I was really concerned. I think the French in their hotel must have been laughing like hell and thinking what a cakewalk they would have."

That may have been precisely the undoing of the French, though they also had other things on their minds. In jail in Christchurch at the time was Dominique Prieur, one of the two French saboteurs of the Greenpeace ship *Rainbow Warrior* in Auckland Harbour the year before. Things French were not a flash flavour at the time and though the French rugby team manager, Yves Noe, did his best to distance his team from the politics, reporters were as keen to talk to French rugby players about terrorism as they were to talk to New Zealand players about apartheid. Noe undertook, not all that wisely, to visit Prieur in Christchurch prison, and did so. Though the players were not involved, such a distraction would not have helped their preparation for a test match.

Across town at the All Blacks' hotel, Lochore detected that his players were nervous and apprehensive, but certainly couldn't be accused of thinking about anything other than the game. They were almost overwhelmed by what they were being asked to do.

"I spent a lot of time chatting to players, individually and collectively, just trying to ease their tension and telling them that all they were being asked to do was what they did best, play rugby. The Friday training was a bit better and I sensed by the Friday night that things were starting to jell, there was a warm feeling and, for the first time, I thought we had a chance. The day before, I'd thought it was impossible."

For all the newness of the team, there was experience and there was natural talent and ambition that would cast a long shadow on All Black rugby in years to come. The newest of the new was the hooker, Sean Fitzpatrick, who had been Lochore's Colts captain two years before. The original choice, Bruce Hemara, had been injured and Fitzpatrick was flown south as a replacement. It was a fortuitous beginning to one of the most remarkable of All Black careers.

Lochore looked at his fresh-faced players in the hotel meeting room on the morning of the match: Greg Cooper, then from Auckland. John Kirwan, by comparison a "veteran", and his Marist and Auckland teammate, Terry Wright. Bearded Joe Stanley from Auckland. Arthur Stone, then from the Bay of Plenty and an All Black in 1981. The gifted Frano Botica from the new North Harbour union. The halfback and captain, David Kirk, who sixty years earlier would have been from the *Chariots of Fire* mould. A talent of rare promise at number eight, Mike Brewer of Otago. The flankers, Mark Brooke-Cowden of Auckland and Brett Harvey of Wairarapa-Bush, an old Lochore ally. The locks, rugged and the type who get called raw-boned, Andy Earl of Canterbury and Gordon Macpherson of Otago. The props, Kevin Boroevich of Wellington and late of King Country, already an All Black but this was his first test, and Brian McGrattan of Wellington, who had been in Argentina the year before.

The reserves were there too: Murray Davie from Canterbury, Iain Abercrombie from Auckland, Joe Leota from Canterbury, Brent Anderson from Wairarapa-Bush, Dean Kenny from Otago and the unfortunate Hemara.

Lochore looked at them. He was proud of those who had gone before in the black jerseys with the silver fern, those who had established and continued a tradition of playing excellence that belongs to few teams in any sport. He told his players that Christchurch morning, June 28, 1986, of that tradition, of what it meant to wear the jersey that they would soon pull on, some for the first time. He told them they would be playing for their mothers, their fathers, their wives, their friends, for all New Zealanders, and for those who had gone before . . . that noble line of men who had crafted, fashioned, moulded what it meant to be an All Black, the name that evokes pride in every New Zealander and strikes fear in the heart of every opponent. He told them they had nothing to fear, they had nothing to worry about. Put the circumstances of today out of your minds, he told them. You are All Blacks. You are here because you are good enough to be here. I chose you to do a job. I wouldn't have chosen you if I didn't think you could do it.

He told them the French weren't bogeymen, they aren't from some super rugby race. They can be beaten. They are just men, just like you. They have two arms, two legs and hearts no bigger than yours. When they're tackled, they fall, just like ordinary men. There is a difference though. You wear the All Black jersey. They don't. Show me I wasn't wrong about you. Show me you're worthy of being an All Black. Show me you're not going to be here for just one test. Show me how good an All Black you can be. Show me what you can do.

And how they showed. This French team was a good team,

198

make no mistake. Look through the team today and the names spring out as being from an illustrious French past. Their playing days are now long gone, but they are still names to be recognised, still names to be reckoned with, stitched into the fabric of the pride of French rugby.

Lochore sat in the grandstand at Lancaster Park and watched his players with that deep satisfaction of knowing they were doing what was needed. He was proud of them. If he was a demonstrative sort of man, he might have hugged them all that day when they walked their light steps back into the dressing room. He might have hugged them all anyway. Cooper the goalkicker, Botica the dropkicker, Brewer the try-scorer who seemed to think that a rugby match was just one endless tackle with lineouts and scrums thrown in for variety, Kirk the director, Earl and Macpherson the leapers . . . every damn one of them.

That night, a sub-editor on the *8 O'Clock*, the old *Auckland Star* Saturday night edition, had an inspired moment and called them "Baby Blacks" in a headline. The name was perfect. It struck a chord. It stuck. Some players in later years didn't like it much, some of the Cavaliers certainly didn't like it, but it encapsulated all the glory of that win and invested in it for evermore the qualities of a David beating a Goliath.

Fairytales come to an end, and a week later in Wellington the mood of Christchurch could not be repeated. Australia, whose coach Alan Jones scoffed at suggestions the All Blacks were an inferior team because so many "top" players were missing (Jones was no fool, he knew that an inferior All Black team is a rare commodity indeed) won by a point, but won. That was all they needed.

"I think by the match at Athletic Park," Lochore recalled, "the focus had moved a little and that's all it needs to lose a test. I think some of our players were looking beyond the match against Australia to when the Cavaliers would again be available for selection, they were looking over their shoulders, and they were wondering about their security in the team. That's fatal for a player. There was also an enormous amount of speculation in the papers about who would be there for the second test and that sort of thing doesn't help the players either. The All Blacks worked hard in Wellington, but there just wasn't the spark there had been against France. Christchurch may have been a oncer, but what a great oncer!"

There was, after the team to play Australia in the second test had been named, considerable criticism that Lochore, Hill and Meads had over-reacted to the one-point loss in Wellington or taken too much advantage of the availability of the Cavaliers. They made ten changes but this was reduced to nine when Wayne Shelford broke a bone in a hand during a club match and Mike Brewer was reprieved. The other Baby Blacks survivors were Cooper, Kirwan, Stanley, Botica and Kirk.

Lochore does not recall any feeling of over-compensating among the selections and said although some of the changes were discussed at length, the discussions were without rancour and there was no split along the lines of "Babies" or Cavaliers. Neither at that point did Lochore detect any ill-feeling among the players, either in the days before the second test in Dunedin or the night of it, when the Wallabies had been beaten by a point, a reversal of the scores in Wellington. In truth, Australia probably should have won because number eight Steve Tuynman scored what seemed a perfectly legitimate try near the terrace corner at the railway embankment end of Carisbrook, only for Welsh referee Derek Bevan not to give it. (This had a humorous sequel a decade later when, in 1996, Tuynman did score, in almost the exact same spot, for former Wallabies against a team of former All Blacks in a match that was a feature of the Masters Games. Justice was done that day, the try was allowed, but the match was drawn.)

In the competitive world of elite sport, it would have been surprising, even astonishing, if the Cavaliers had returned to the fold and everything just carried on as before, all united in the All Black cause and anxiously and quickly putting aside differences.

Inevitably, this did not happen. By the time of the final test in Auckland, ill feeling was apparent to those close to the team such as Lochore. It had not, and did not till years later, become a public issue. There was a feeling, from both sides, of "them" and "us". On the one side, some of the Cavaliers regarded the others as usurpers; on the other side, some of the Baby Blacks resented the implication they weren't good enough to be All Blacks in their own right.

A particular target was David Kirk, the captain who had decided against joining the Cavaliers the year before. Some of the Cavaliers questioned his motives, but if Kirk withdrew from the South African trip so as not to jeopardise his Rhodes Scholarship, he could hardly be blamed. It would have seemed a perfectly natural, and prudent, thing to do.

"By Auckland, there was more feeling than I thought," Lochore recalled. "I thought I was dealing just with rugby players but there was more to it than that. Some players had their own agendas. Nothing was ever reported directly to me but it was evident there was quite strong feeling between some of the players. I had to remind them that they were all All Blacks in the same team and that they were playing for their country together. I think there was probably outside pressure on some of them as well. The Cavaliers had read opinions that the Baby Blacks should have been there and it made preparing for a test match more difficult psychologically for them. I heard of one or two spats between players but they never amounted to anything and in fact may have cleared the air a little.

"Though the test match was lost, it was lost because we tried to play an expansive game and made too many mistakes while the Wallabies played it cautiously and won. I think the All Blacks, given their riding instructions, just went too far, tried to run when it wasn't on, that sort of thing. It was a bit ironic really, since it's the Aussies who are always saying it's them who play expansively and we're conservative. I don't think, even with a decade of hindsight, that the Cavaliers-Babies business had any effect on the field. Not at all.

"It was, I suppose, a matter of readjustment for both lots after a couple of very trying years and it was probably inevitable among very competitive sports people that something would develop. In the end, they settled their differences and got on with what they knew they had to do."

9

ON TOP OF THE WORLD

Among the hoariest of hoary cliches is that it is an ill wind that blows no good and that an unhappy event is a blessing in disguise. No-one in Nantes, the capital of the Pays de la Loire economic region in western France, had either of those cliches in mind on the night of November 15, 1986. No New Zealanders anyway, and none of the New Zealanders at home either who had watched the All Blacks get thumped 16-3 in the second international on the end-of-season tour.

The All Blacks were well beaten, beaten out of sight, thrashed. Brian Lochore thought that if a team could come third in a rugby match, the All Blacks that day would have been third.

The total eclipse of New Zealand's favourite sons was all the more surprising and unpalatable because it was so unexpected. The All Blacks' tour of France had otherwise been stunningly successful, setting a variety of points-scoring records, included a dominant 19-7 win over France in the first test in Toulouse – in front of such a poor crowd that Toulouse was not to host another New Zealand test for a decade – and, perhaps most important of all, had healed what rifts there were among the players after the "them" and "us" tensions of earlier in the year. All that was needed, it seemed, was a winning second test to cap a successful tour. Alas.

But this was where the cliches came in. After the disappointment and the empty feeling in the stomach that All Blacks get when they lose had passed, it was a time for reflection and for looking forward. The World Cup was to be in New Zealand and Australia the following year and, in fact, the All

Blacks would not have another test until their cup opener against Italy at Eden Park on May 22. Nantes became a rallying call, the battlecry of "Remember Nantes!" echoing through New Zealand's preparations for rugby's first World Cup.

Complacency is not a word that figures often among All Blacks and there was none in 1986, but Nantes brought home to the players in the most graphic way possible that a team they beat one week can just as easily reverse the order the following week and that no team, but no team, can be taken lightly. And it wasn't as if the All Blacks in Nantes had taken the French lightly, not by conscious thought anyway. What Nantes did was to sharpen and focus the All Blacks' resolve.

"The All Blacks were shattered by that loss," Lochore said. "It was the best thing to happen in terms of the World Cup. Had we won, even by six points, we would have been seen as favourites for the World Cup. Players would have gone home and spent the summer lying around on beaches and not thinking of the work they would still have to do. France did us an incredible favour. We were wounded Kiwis. Our pride was wounded."

The French tour had other benefits. It laid to rest the South African bogey and never again would that festering issue of New Zealand rugby dominate thinking. The issue of whether to play or not against South Africa was in the past.

There had been some murmurings, public and private, after the team for France had been named that Lochore making Jock Hobbs the captain in place of David Kirk, whose star had risen with the Baby Blacks, was a sop to the returned rebels, a transparent effort to meld the two camps of All Black rugby into one. This was not so.

"Jock had been captain in Argentina the year before," Lochore recalled, "we'd got on very well and I had confidence in his ability to captain a touring side. The choice of a captain for a tour is much more crucial than a captain for a home test, much more is required of the captain. Jock had experience as a captain on tour and David did not. The decision when it was made was based on that experience, not on personalities. And the Cavaliers factor quite simply was not a factor."

The simmering feeling between the Cavaliers and the "Babies" that had been evident during the series against Australia dissipated on tour, as Lochore knew it would. He'd toured often enough as a player to know that New Zealanders in general, and All Blacks in particular, stick together on tours, that they work happily together for their common goals, and that anything that had gone before was forgotten. New Zealanders and Australians are possibly better tourists than any other rugby country – the cliques and other discordant factors on British and French tours have rarely been evident on an All Black tour, if ever.

The French tour also gave Lochore a happy dilemma: whether to play Grant Fox, the gifted kicking five-eighth, or Frano Botica, the brilliant running five-eighth, in the tests. It was a dilemma any coach would be happy to face and one that was eventually resolved with Fox becoming the greatest points-scorer New Zealand rugby has known, and one of its greatest tacticians, and Botica, frustrated, seeking out new challenges in league, which he met with all the skill and talent that rugby people knew he had. In France, though, Lochore opted for Botica because he thought his running skills, allied with a kicking game that any other country would be proud to have, gave the All Blacks more options.

Early in the tour, Fox could see from the way teams were being selected that Lochore was likely to pick Botica for the tests, and Botica had had the inside running by playing in each of the domestic tests. Lochore recalls Fox approaching him around the time of the game in Perpignan, two matches before the first test, and asking in the direct manner that Fox has: "BJ, what do I have to do to get a test?"

Lochore was as direct as Fox: "Foxy, you've just got to play better."

He went on to tell Fox that Botica offered extra options

because of his instinctive running game and because he was expert at backing up, getting round on the outside of his centre and wings.

Fox nodded and went off to training.

The next game, against a Cote Basque team in Bayonne, he played a blinder. "He ran everything and he played exceedingly well," Lochore recalled. "It was an amazing transformation. It was the best possible response Foxy could make."

Lochore stuck to Botica for the Toulouse test and then Fox's response was rendered academic. He collapsed the night of the Toulouse test and spent a few days in hospital being treated for a collapsed lung, the lingering and painful result of a Steven Pokere tackle earlier in the year. It was the end of Fox's tour of France.

He wasn't the only casualty. The two test props, John Drake and Steve McDowell, both had niggling injuries and Lochore had to call in Richard Loe, then playing for Lyon, to make his All Black debut in the between-tests match against the Barbarians in La Rochelle. The front row injuries didn't help the New Zealand cause in Nantes, but that wasn't an excuse. A convalescing Fox sat with Lochore in the Stade de la Beaujoire in Nantes and watched France deal to the All Blacks. "They were ruthless," Lochore recalled. "They just overran us in the forwards. It was one of the most complete forward displays I've ever seen. The whole team just ran at us. They were quite different from what they had been the week before."

Lochore at the after-match press conference referred, in his laconic New Zealand way, to the French turnaround being so complete it was almost as if they were on drugs. It was a comment that would return to briefly haunt, then humour, him.

Back home a few weeks later, Lochore received a phone call from Chris Thau, a likeable Romanian who had covered the tour for the British *Rugby World* magazine. An unholy row had broken out in France, Thau told Lochore, because of the throwaway line about drugs.

"They're saying you accused the French of being on drugs and now there's talk of having a full inquiry," Thau, who is fluent in French, told Lochore.

"But it was tongue in cheek," Lochore protested.

"I know that," Thau said, "and the New Zealand and British journalists know that, but something must have got lost in the translation or the French didn't understand the New Zealand humour."

Concerned, Lochore phoned Sylvie Gentry at the New Zealand Rugby Union in Wellington and arranged for her to write a letter of explanation, in careful French, to the president of the French federation, Albert Ferrasse. The explanation was gratefully accepted by the French, of course, and the furore died down as quickly as it had risen.

France was a revelation to Lochore in a non-rugby sense as well. He'd toured there as a player in 1964 and '67 and hadn't been impressed. "If I didn't like it for ten days or so on those tours," he thought, "it's going to be hell for five or six weeks."

But if not a heaven, it wasn't hell either. "It had changed enormously," he recalled, "and was a pleasure to tour. More people spoke English than appeared to be the case from what I remembered, they were much more affluent generally, the hotels were of a much higher standard. It was a pleasure to tour there, the changes were phenomenal."

Language is always a problem on a tour where English is not the first language. The lack of easy and automatic communication can turn minor problems into major problems and turn humour into vexed frustration. What helped in 1986, and even more on later tours of France in 1990 and '95, was the number of All Blacks who spoke French, a by-product of the increasing number of players who have spent a season or two with clubs there.

The tour marked the last appearance for New Zealand of Mark Shaw, the flanker whose reputation for being a hard man diminished and detracted from the enormous contributions he made as an All Black, especially on a tour. Many All Blacks would give a figurative right arm to play for their country but in Shaw's case if it was necessary it would have been a literal right arm, assuming the physical disability could be overcome. He was a hard man yes, and he stood for no nonsense on the rugby field, but he was also the type of ideal player, on the field and off it, that any coach would pick first.

"He was misunderstood by a good many New Zealanders," Lochore said. "I think the public probably knew or saw only the hard side, but he would do anything for anyone and he was an asset on tour. He was one of the most dedicated All Blacks I've been associated with and he'd prepare for a game like almost no-one else. There's a lot of players who could learn an awful lot from Cowboy Shaw."

Lochore showed what he thought of Shaw by making him the All Blacks' midweek captain on three occasions, including the significant second-last match, against the French Barbarians.

"He did a terrific job," Lochore said simply.

It wasn't long after the French tour that the New Zealand union re-elected Lochore its convenor of the selection panel and chose, for the first time, his co-panelists Alex Wyllie and John Hart. There was no surprise about that. Wyllie and Hart had been the two dominant provincial coaches for the past three or four years and when both in 1986 made their interest in the national job known, it was almost a foregone conclusion that they would join Lochore.

Hart had revitalised Auckland rugby since taking over as coach in 1982 and gradually built a side that would become acknowledged as one of the best provincial teams ever seen in New Zealand, if not the best. Wyllie had worked similar magic in Canterbury, taking over at rather a moribund period then winning the Ranfurly Shield from Wellington and keeping it till that epic encounter in Christchurch in 1985 against Auckland.

Auckland and Canterbury were far and away the best two teams in New Zealand (though Wellington under Earle Kirton had won the national championship in 1986) and now their coaches were charged, under Lochore's stewardship, with winning the first World Cup for New Zealand.

The new panel got together for the first time one night in Wellington two days after being elected. It was immediately apparent to Lochore, and he thinks to the others, that there was a rapport between them and that they had strikingly similar views about rugby and how they wanted it played and, most importantly, how they thought the All Blacks should play to win the cup.

"We totally agreed on how we ought to play and we all appreciated the style of expansive play that we thought was not only the formula for winning rugby, but also for entertaining rugby," Lochore recalled.

"We knew we didn't have big enough forwards to foot it with the French or the English or the Australians and we knew we had to use all our skills and our rugby know-how. We agreed immediately we had to pick the players to suit the type of game we wanted rather than impose a style on players, but we knew as well that we would be picking pretty much all of the current players."

An earlier All Black coach, Jack Gleeson, once said that his ideal for a rugby player was one who would play the game at pace and be a thinker. That was precisely what Lochore, Wyllie and Hart wanted. To play successfully and accurately the type of game they wanted, players would have to be supremely fit, fitter than the All Blacks had ever been. Wyllie in Canterbury had used the conditioning skills of a Scottish-born Auckland fitness instructor, Jim Blair. It had returned such handsome dividends for Canterbury that Hart paid Wyllie the compliment by also using Blair, who became something of a fitness guru in rugby.

It was both necessary and inevitable that Blair was among the first people Lochore approached. Get the All Blacks fit and ready to peak in May, was the firm instruction. Lochore, Wyllie and Hart drew up a list of about 50 players – their names were never made public but they included all who would eventually be in the World Cup squad – to be put on tailored fitness programmes by Blair. Such a practice was an innovation in early 1987. It was to become the norm for international teams as soon as other countries saw that precisely conditioned All Blacks were even more formidable than All Blacks traditionally were.

"Jim Blair did individual fitness programmes for each of the players and he sent me assessment forms every so often, keeping me informed about the progress of each player," Lochore recalled. "But in the end, we didn't really need the assessment forms because we picked on form, knowing that each All Black was as fit as he could be.

"The players we were most worried about were those who were not getting early-season rugby in the South Pacific championship, and that meant players from outside Canterbury, Auckland and Wellington. We were very concerned about some guys not getting enough games and we arranged a trial match especially for players not involved in the South Pacific."

April was the month of decision for the three selectors and it was the month in which players could sway decisions. It began with the trial in Hamilton, when a team of Possibles led by Mike Brewer beat a team of Probables led by Mark Shaw, and continued with the introduction of the short-lived inter-zonal series, when the North, Central and South zones played for the specially made George Nepia Memorial Trophy, a handsome prize carved from totara and in memory of one of the greatest of All Blacks. If the zone series was not a success in itself, it nevertheless, in 1987 at least, served as a useful series of trials, reminiscent of the forties and fifties when there were North and South Island trials, culminating in a final trial that was seen as a test dress rehearsal.

Lochore, Wyllie and Hart travelled, watched, analysed and discussed throughout April as they and a legion of unofficial selectors drew up their World Cup squad of 26. Unlike many or most of the unofficial selectors, the three real ones had early on worked out the reality of the World Cup: that it was a test series of a maximum of six matches and could not be looked upon as a tour. The best XV would have to be fielded in each match and the squad of 26 had to be picked with that in mind, so in effect it was a three-level squad: test team, six reserves and five others who could cover key positions. It took other countries the example of New Zealand and another four years to reach this conclusion.

By the time the final trial in early May in Whangarei was reached, 13 days before the World Cup opener against Italy, the squad was committed to the minds of each of the selectors. The match in Whangarei, from which some squad certainties such as David Kirk and Gary Whetton had been rested, served more to confirm the selectors' thinking than it did to give them fresh ideas.

Not that the rest of New Zealand saw things in such a clear-cut way. It had been arranged, through television and rugby's new-found sponsorship with Steinlager, for the trial teams to be at dinner at the Grand Hotel in Whangarei and the squad would be announced, during the dinner, live on television. It was some time after the trial and the public, and those journalists who were in Whangarei, assumed that the selectors in the interim period would be ensconced in their hotel room anguishing over their final selections. Not so.

"It was the quickest team to be named of any I was associated with," Lochore said. "We thought that if it was named too quickly people would think we were not serious enough so we had to fill in a bit of time."

Rather than pencilling in names and rubbing others out, debating and deliberating, the three selectors were actually on the floor. Hart had a sore back and, after some discussion of methods, Wyllie and Lochore decided to treat Hart themselves.

Hart lay compliantly on the floor while, as Lochore described it, the two of them gave him some old-fashioned Chinese treatment. "He did have a genuinely sore back and we were trying to help him, but there was a bit of hilarity as well with Harty on the floor and Alex and I sitting on him and 'manipulating' him."

There was serious discussion at the meeting too and it mostly concerned the final choice between the two Anderson locks, Albert from Canterbury and Brent from Wairarapa-Bush. The Canterbury Anderson was finally chosen because of his greater lineout ability, but each of the selectors felt desperately sorry for Brent Anderson, who had played marvellously well in his solid, committed way in the zone and trial matches. Later that night, each of the selectors individually went to Brent Anderson to console and explain.

The method of announcing the cup squad had something of the quality of a meat market about it. Players, officials and journalists were sitting having dinner at the Grand Hotel as the team was announced and as television cameras roamed around the room, picking out the faces of the elated and the dejected, the happy and the sad. Team announcements have seldom been handled well in New Zealand and little consideration has been given to players' feelings, but this was one of the more public exposures. Most players would feel it is a private moment and they should be left alone in their joy or depression or with family or close friends.

"I didn't like that announcement though I understood well enough the reasons for doing it that way," Lochore said. "It's a hard time for the players and it doesn't make it any easier when it's in the public gaze like that. That announcement was even more special because it was an historic occasion, being the first World Cup squad."

The captain, to no-one's surprise, was Andy Dalton. He hadn't captained the All Blacks since the test against Australia in 1985 and had missed almost all of the 1986 season because of the broken jaw he suffered in South Africa, but the selectors were of one mind about who should lead New Zealand in such an important campaign. Their thinking was plain for all to see when he was named as captain of the North zone team and again captain in the final trial. The selectors' decision was made easier by the retirement during the summer of the captain in France, Jock Hobbs.

Dalton, who had been an All Black since 1977, was vastly experienced in all the various roles a captain must bring to his team and he had the respect of all the players, partly because of his playing ability and the way he had adapted to the elevated hooker's role as an extra loose forward, but partly because of his wisdom and manner off the field. He was a natural leader.

But fate was to deal him a cruel blow. About a week after the final trial and the naming of the squad, the players assembled in Auckland – with the squads from the other eleven countries – but without their coach, Brian Lochore, and the two Wellington players, John Gallagher and Murray Pierce. Wellington airport had been fogged in and Lochore rang Dalton at the Poenamo on the North Shore, the All Blacks' perennial home away from home in Auckland, told him he'd been delayed and that Dalton should take the squad for a light training.

"Make sure they all do their stretches and then just have a light run, I'll see you when I get there," the coach told his captain.

It was a grim-faced Dalton who greeted Lochore at the Poenamo late in the afternoon. "I've done a hamstring," Dalton said. "How bad?" Lochore asked. "Not too bad, but I'm worried," Dalton said.

Not too bad? Bad enough. Amazingly, the news of the crocked captain didn't immediately reach the hundreds of journalists who had gathered in Auckland for the cup opening. No conscious decision had been made to keep the injury quiet, but equally, as Lochore said, "We didn't hang a sign around his neck, saying 'I'm injured'."

The news filtered out as it became apparent that Dalton wasn't training with the team then the import of it was driven fully home when Lochore named his strongest side for the cup opener and had Kirk as captain and Sean Fitzpatrick at hooker.

The official word was that Dalton might be out for one or two games but would definitely remain one of the squad. In fact, remain as captain rather than "one of". As the tournament wore on though, it became evident that even if Dalton's wayward hamstring could withstand the rigours of an eighty-minute test match on top of full training runs, there would be an element of risk that he was out of match fitness.

Dalton, when he saw the futility, told Lochore he would go home if that was what would be best for the team. "Not on your life," Lochore told him. "You're the captain. You're staying."

Dalton smiled at the ribbing he took from other players about being the non-playing captain, but it must have been hard for him to be the leader of men, but not part of them. Lochore was full of admiration and praise for the way Dalton conducted himself and carried on with his duties as captain as if he was still leader on the field.

"The upfront image of the All Blacks was David Kirk. He was the player most people related to and he became the image of All Black rugby in 1987, but there was no doubt in the minds of anyone in the squad, including David, about who the captain was. Andy was the complete captain for the whole time except for the six times eighty minutes they were on the field. David took over the minute they ran out and Andy took over the minute they came back."

It wasn't exactly planned that way. The tradition in All Black rugby is that the last few minutes, perhaps five or so, in the dressing room before a match are for the 15 players who are about to take the field. The coach and the reserves head for the grandstand, other team officials head elsewhere. It's the time for the captain to make his last-minute entreaties to his players, the time for players to reassure and support one another. So it was at Eden Park for the first match against Italy. Dalton sat in the stand while Kirk was down below in the dressing room in the final moments. But thereafter, for each of the cup games including the final, Dalton stayed with the players till the referee's knock on the door, till the players' last words and till they emerged from the shadows into the sunlight of their successes.

"You could now, nearly ten years later, go to any one of the 1987 World Cup All Blacks and ask them who the captain was and each would say without hesitation that it was Andy Dalton," Lochore says.

It was a publicly touching moment after the final therefore when Kirk, after holding the cup aloft, beckoned to Dalton to stand with him and share the moment. But it was, privately, an even more telling moment. It was Kirk acknowledging who had led them through the campaign.

It was a long campaign, it was arduous and it was, for rugby players, unprecedented. The prize went to the team and the players who planned it best, prepared for it best, understood it best and, of course, played it best. On every count, the All Blacks stood supreme.

These things don't just happen. Lochore doesn't just say to his players, "Get out there and throw it around." There's a great deal of tactical and strategical planning, but there's also a great deal of what might be called psychological planning. Rugby players are like people anywhere. They can get bored with the familiar, they can get upset with a different routine, they have emotions like anyone, they like and dislike, laugh and cry. These All Blacks were as much a cross-section of New Zealanders as any other group of 26 New Zealanders. What they had in common was an uncommon ability to play rugby well. It was Lochore's job, and Hart and Wyllie's, to get them to play as well as they possibly could and, perhaps most significantly, to create the environment in which they could perform at their best on their home stage.

An essential element of the success in 1987 was the harmony among the selection panel. Once the squad had been chosen, there was no formal role left for Wyllie or Hart. Each was a selector, but neither was an assistant coach. Lochore was in sole charge, he never asked the New Zealand union for an assistant. But it would have been ludicrous for Lochore not to utilise the skills available, especially when the tournament was at home. So Lochore, Wyllie and Hart all turned up at an early training run in Auckland in tracksuits and boots. There was no doubt who the boss was, but it became a little confusing after that.

"I'd made it clear to them that I wanted them to be a part of it all. They were a great asset to me, we all worked well together and they knew the players very well since a fair percentage of them were from Auckland or Canterbury.

"But we got back to our hotel from that training run and agreed it was hopeless. There were too many of us there. The players were confused, there were too many mixed messages although none of that, of course, was deliberate. So I said we should split up. John would help at trainings in the North Island and Alex would help in the South Island. It seemed the ideal solution and it worked. It also helped inject freshness into training and in a tournament such as the World Cup when there are no midweek games between tests, the players need all the variety they can get otherwise boredom and staleness can set in."

Lochore's realisation of the need for variety, as much as his rugby planning, contributed to the success. Before the Argentina match in Wellington, for example, Lochore tried something completely different by dispatching his players for a night to Pirinoa, a rural community in southern Wairarapa. Andy Earl came from there and between he and Lochore, they probably knew every family in the area and got on the phone and arranged accommodation. When Lochore explained the arrangements to the players and told them they would be staying with local families, there were a few groans. "The thought of being billeted was a bit too much for some of them," Lochore said. "They thought they were a bit beyond that sort of thing. I'd originally planned for a couple of nights but when I saw the players' reactions I thought, 'Gee, maybe I've gone too far, maybe I'd better make it one night'."

Significant ruin – Lochore Castle, Fife.

Winners of the Christie Cup for Central Districts tennis.

Pam with my mother, father and a light breakfast.

A study in rural serenity. David, Pam, Sandra and Joanne.

Ross Setford, Fotopacific

Half-time chat with "Baby Blacks" Michael Speight and Brent Anderson, 1986 v Australia.

John Blackwell, Collection

World Cup final, 1987.

The Cup floweth over. World Cup 1987.

Other pursuits, Johannesburg, 1995.

John Selkirk

The other side of touring life.

John Selkirk

Lomu press conference, team hotel Pretoria, 1995.

Addressing the troops, World Cup 1995.

Three generations . . . with Jeff Wilson and Sean Fitzpatrick.

John Selkirk

Brian Lochore joins the team on field before the first World Cup match v Ireland at Ellis Park.

So one night it was and the players thoroughly enjoyed themselves. Mainly city folk, as country people called them, they revelled in the rural lifestyle by driving tractors or four-wheel motorbikes, duck shooting or other pursuits that are part of the daily life of people who are not surrounded by cars and concrete. "They had a ball and would have loved to stay the extra night," Lochore recalled.

Another relaxing innovation was that when the squad was in Auckland, the Aucklanders were allowed to stay at home except for the night before the match, and so it applied too for Gallagher and Pierce in Wellington and for the Cantabrians in Christchurch. It was all part of the variety and the break-up of routine.

When the team was in Christchurch for the Scotland quarterfinal, they had a training session at Little River on Banks Peninsula, an area of no great rugby distinction although it could claim Tom Robinson, of the 1926-27 New Zealand Maori team that toured Britain and France, as one of its own. Lochore felt for two of the All Blacks, Bruce Deans and Frano Botica, who to that point had not played and, as it turned out, would not play a game. So he told the two of them, plus all except those who had been named to play the quarterfinal, to take a night off and spend it in Akaroa and they could do what they wanted provided they had one hard run. This they did and they returned to the All Blacks' Christchurch hotel the next day refreshed and thankful that Lochore was not thinking only of the 15 "main" players.

Part of the selection process had been to choose players who the selectors thought could withstand the different pressures of being an All Black but not actually playing. Other unique pressures of the cup were, in effect, touring your own country where everything is familiar, players had been to the hotels many times before, the training grounds were the same, they knew which showers had only cold water and they knew which bench in a changing room had a loose board. Another pressure of playing at home is the constant recognition and the continued close contact with family and friends, all of which can serve to detract from the prime task.

Even the coaches had their variety. At the formal opening dinner in Auckland, Lochore had been introduced to the Romanian captain, Mircea Paraschiv, who immediately asked if Lochore could give them some assistance at training the next day. He happily obliged, knowing that he was not giving away All Black secrets and that Romania were in a different pool and not likely to pose a later threat to New Zealand. Similarly, Wyllie in Christchurch took the Italian forwards through an excruciating and exhaustive session of scrummaging at Rugby Park – and it has to be said that this was after the All Blacks had played Italy.

One of the funnier moments of the World Cup was an Italian lock, sweating and heaving profusely and his jersey sodden with sweat, poking his head out of a scrum and saying in his best English, "Please Mr Wyllie, not one more!"

The Italians were delightful and quick learners, but the All Blacks also saw them as a threat. It was in 1987, as it has always been, a creed of the All Blacks that the team you take lightly is the team that will beat you.

"We couldn't afford to take any team easily because when you do, it's the day you lose," Lochore said. "It's not in our nature to go into a game thinking it will be easy. The press may think the All Blacks will win without a problem and the public may think the same, but the All Blacks will never do that. They wouldn't be All Blacks if they did."

So Italy was dealt with mercilessly in the first, historic game, a game that not only set the tone of the World Cup but set a standard for the All Blacks. It was the sort of opening that Lochore wanted and he exhorted his players to maintain that standard for the rest of the tournament, not that they needed much telling. It's a truism of All Blacks that they play out of their skins not only because of their opponents, but because they know if they don't there are six reserves sitting in the stand, and others elsewhere, who would happily take their places.

It's a truism also, as well as the most repetitive of cliches, that All Blacks take each game as it comes, as they must. To lift the sights beyond the next opponent is to invite disaster. The All Blacks had this drummed into them by Lochore as they played and beat Fiji in Christchurch, then played and beat Argentina in Wellington. Lochore was able to lift his sights and look at threats on the horizon and he was worried about the Pumas. He remembered how competitive they had been in 1985 and they still had the maestro, Hugo Porta, getting on in years but still able to change the course of a match with one twinkle of an eye or one flick of a boot.

For the first time, Lochore made a few changes for the Argentina match – Zinzan Brooke making his debut on the openside, Richard Loe in the front row, Andy Earl at number eight, Bernie McCahill at second five-eighth, Terry Wright on the wing and Kieran Crowley at fullback – mainly because the All Blacks had already qualified for the quarterfinals, but partly because he didn't want too many players not having a game. The biggest worry that day at Athletic Park was, as it turned out, not the Pumas but the captain, David Kirk. The Pumas had been well subdued late in the game when Kirk was hit by a rampaging late tackle that flattened him. Alarmed, a couple of the All Blacks quickly escorted Kirk off the field. Was he concussed? Would he have to stand down for three weeks? The medical opinion was that he was not and, though shaken and stirred, Kirk was fit to play again in a couple of days. Lochore was a relieved man. He did not want to contemplate the prospect of a third captain.

Though the All Blacks focused on their own game and gave only passing attention to the others, they were at Lancaster Park when Scotland drew with France on the second day of the tournament, much the same France who had beaten the All Blacks the year before in Nantes. They felt the Scots were the better team that day and, on the form they'd since shown, were one of the more formidable sides in the tournament. The Scots should have won. They prepared for the quarterfinal in

Christchurch as if it was the only game in their lives that mattered. To lose would be to go home. There could be nothing more galling for a host country at the first World Cup than to watch the final stages on television.

One of Lochore's most cutting lines to the players, a line they happily repeated, was: "Do we want to go back to work on Monday?"

It was this fear that added the turbocharger to the rocket fuel they were already playing on. The Scots, as brave and determined as Scots always are, were annihilated. Their captain, Colin Deans, said the game just seemed to be one endless attempted tackle of a white jersey (the All Blacks had played in white to avoid a clash with Scotland's blue). He had nothing but admiration for the All Blacks, though they'd been beaten 30-3. The All Blacks, for their part, later felt that Scotland were the second-best team in the cup. Deans was in no doubt who would win the final, but the All Blacks had other things on their mind.

"Looking back, the match against Scotland was probably our best game of the whole tournament," Lochore recalled. "But at the time it was just another step, and the next step was Wales. Maybe not the Wales of times past, but still Wales."

Rather than go to Brisbane immediately for the semifinal, Lochore, again in the name of variety, took the All Blacks to Napier for two nights. They trained at the Maori Agricultural College at Te Aute where they were given a Maori welcome and watched by the rugby-mad schoolboys. It was the sort of environment that fuelled the nationalism the All Blacks were already feeling. They trained too in front of a crowd of about 5000 at McLean Park. It was supposed to have been a light training but as is often the case when a crowd shows up, the players think they have to do more. So they did, till Lochore had to restrain them.

Once in Brisbane, things did not go well. "Coaching a side in the World Cup is, I imagine, like training a racehorse for a Melbourne Cup three weekends in succession. You sense when things are going right and when things are going wrong and you've got to get the balance just right. We had a light run in Brisbane on the Thursday and, because it was a Sunday game, our main training was on the Friday. But it did not go well. Their minds were just not there.

"So we had another run on the Saturday morning and things were a lot better. Their minds were back again."

That afternoon, Australia and France were playing in the first semifinal at Concord Oval in Sydney. Lochore assembled his players in a hotel meeting room to watch the game on television. The room was big and the television set was small. Only the players in the front row could see anything. Lochore told the players to go to their rooms to watch.

"We hadn't discussed the match at all. We hadn't talked about who we wanted to win and who we wanted to meet in the final. The reason, of course, was that we still had our semifinal to play and you can't go thinking about the final till you've won the semi. I could of course, but the players couldn't."

"So everyone went to their rooms to watch the game and as is the way with rugby teams, we were all in the same area of the hotel and players left their doors open. When France scored their last-minute try to win, a great roar echoed along the corridor. There was no doubt then who the players wanted to meet in the final."

Wales the next day at Ballymore were a disappointment. They had nothing like the firepower or commitment needed to stay a team in such a rampant mood as the All Blacks. New Zealand's 49-6 win could have been more. New Zealand could also have lost the number eight, Wayne Shelford. Ten minutes from the end, Welsh lock Huw Richards indulged in some thuggery and Shelford retaliated, much more effectively than Richards' initial thrust had been. Richards was semi-conscious on the ground when referee Kerry Fitzgerald ordered him from the field. In later years, Shelford might have been ordered off too.

"I saw what Buck did and I could see why he did it, but

229

I wasn't happy," Lochore said. "I don't like that sort of thing. But I breathed a sigh of relief when no action was taken against him."

Back to Auckland. Back for the final. The end of a long road. Time to exorcise the ghosts of Nantes. Time to exorcise other ghosts. Time to prove, after years of unofficial reckonings, the All Blacks were the best in the world.

Again, the training before the final was not great. "The players were just not there," Lochore said. "France, because they had played on the Saturday, had an extra day on us and that makes a difference in a five-week tournament."

Lochore took the All Blacks to King's College, a distinguished Auckland school and alma mater of Ian Kirkpatrick, on the Friday. This time they were ready. "I hardly needed to say anything, I could hardly stop them," Lochore said. "They were ready for the final. There was nothing more I could do. There was nothing anyone could do."

Fifteen All Blacks took the field in the final, eleven more were sitting watching. Twenty-six. There were, perhaps, as many reasons for the way they approached the game, the way they played it, as there were players. Each would have had his own motivation, each had been inculcated with the team's. There was the feeling of union that belongs to any team. But greater than that was the feeling that, for the first time in years, the All Blacks were playing for all New Zealand. There was not an element of society that shunned them, and there was no longer any All Black ashamed of wearing his dress jumper with the silver fern out in public.

"We knew all of New Zealand was behind us," Lochore said. "There was enormous support. We could detect the difference even between the first week of the tournament and the days before the final. The World Cup had captured the country and we were at the heart of it. It put more pressure on us to do well, but we were happy with that because we were playing for all of New Zealand and not just a part of it."

Lochore was only too conscious that David Kirk, the stand-in captain who did such a magnificent job, had become the public face of All Black rugby. "I have no doubt that David's presence, and the boyish looks that people said made a lot of women want to mother him, was a huge factor in the following we received and in putting public opinion on our side. He was seen as the fresh, new face of rugby and as the World Cup itself was the dawn of a new era, then so was the image that David portrayed of the All Blacks."

The morning of the final was like any other test match morning, though it wasn't any other. It was the World Cup final. The first World Cup final. Players were nervous and tense, and that's no bad thing provided they're not too nervous or too tense. Conversation among players was monosyllabic, but that's normal on test match morning. It's not possible to see Eden Park from the Poenamo on the North Shore, but it was in every player's mind's eye. Some players may have thought of the French or their own French opponent. Sella. Blanco. Condom. Mesnel. But most would have thought about their own game, the need to be free of mistakes, the need for speed of thought and of foot, the need to tackle. The need to win.

When the All Blacks walked from the hotel to their bus to take them to Eden Park, a crowd of about 500 cheered them and wished them well. Five hundred! Not yet at Eden Park. As the bus went over the bridge and round the edge of inner Auckland, people waved and cheered, shouted best wishes that were lost in the roar of the exhaust. As Eden Park got nearer, the crowds got thicker. More people cheered. Some just stood and watched with their unspoken prayers.

Lochore saw all this from the bus. "I needn't have bothered with a team talk," he said. "The people of New Zealand were saying it all. It was there for all to see and hear. The players knew. They were playing for the people outside the hotel, the people in the streets, the people outside the park, the people inside, the people at home watching on television. They were playing for all

New Zealanders everywhere. They couldn't let them down. They wouldn't let them down."

They didn't.

For All Blacks, test matches go by in a blur. Any new All Black will say the thing he notices most about his first test is the speed at which it is played. He's hard put later to recall any detail from the game. It becomes instinctive, it's played from the heart. On June 20, 1987, the All Blacks played with speed and heart, they played with verve, they played with elan. They played to win. No team would have beaten the All Blacks that day. France were shut down and out early and anything that France did later was to gain some pride for themselves. It was the All Blacks' day. It was New Zealand rugby's year.

10

A CAMPAIGN THWARTED

The World Cup won, it was time for Brian Lochore to retire. He had no intention of deviating from his original plan of three years as coach and the plan had worked, despite the disruptions of 1985 and '86. The events of 1987 had made it all worthwhile.

There was still some unfinished business though. There was the Bledisloe Cup to be regained in Sydney, and it was regained in style with the score, 30-16, reversing a particular sore point of New Zealand rugby, the 30-16 loss to Australia at Eden Park in 1978 when Greg Cornelsen scored four tries. None of the All Blacks got four on this occasion, but Sean Fitzpatrick was halfway there with two from his newly acquired specialist role as an extra wing.

The match had been billed as being between the two sides that were expected to have played in the World Cup final and the Australians saw it as their chance for redemption. The All Blacks were worried because they had not played for three weeks and they knew the Wallabies, who had made a couple of changes from their cup team including dropping captain Andrew Slack, would be happy to ambush them. Despite the final scoreline, the match was tight and the All Blacks trailed at halftime. Even with ten minutes to go, they led by only a point but it was all New Zealand in that final period and they swept to a majestic victory for which they had had to fight hard, perhaps harder than any of the cup matches.

There was ecstasy at the regaining of the Bledisloe Cup, but the dominant emotion among the New Zealanders after the match was relief that they had not failed at the final hurdle.

There was also, at the end of the season, an All Black tour of Japan that the New Zealand union had decided would be undertaken by something of a B team, though the guidelines for the selectors changed several times, partly because the autocratic ruler of Japanese rugby, Shiggy Kono, did not want anything other than the best All Black team. Lochore had told Wyllie and Hart and the New Zealand union chairman, Russ Thomas, that he was not seeking re-election, but had asked them not to make it public – though the public had a fair idea anyway.

Lochore felt Wyllie or Hart should go to Japan and they discussed it early in the year, agreeing that one should coach the Colts on the internal tour and the other take whatever team was decided to Japan. Hart said he could not get away from this job at Fletcher Challenge at the time of the Colts tour, so Wyllie happily agreed to coach that team, leaving Hart as coach for Japan with Wyllie as his assistant. The Japanese tour was to be the catalyst for a lot of the Wyllie-Hart stories, some true, most of them false, that were to bedevil New Zealand rugby till after the 1991 World Cup.

They could have been avoided, or at least nipped in the bud, if the intention to send a strong All Black team, only a few places different from the World Cup squad, had been plain throughout the year. Lochore would have done the job himself. "If I'd known that the New Zealand union would change its mind and send almost a full-strength team, I would have reconsidered and probably gone myself," Lochore said. "But by the time it was apparent what the team would be, it was already public knowledge that Harty was taking the team. There was nothing I could have done to change it, and because of the agreement we'd already made, I wouldn't have attempted to change it."

Lochore, then, watched from afar when the All Blacks trampled over the pride of Japanese rugby, putting up huge scores and playing some sublime rugby. There were criticisms, or at least qualifications, that the All Blacks were playing "only"

Japan – observations that Lochore would face again in the future – but it's an often overlooked fact that a team that scores a hundred points has to play very well indeed, regardless of the quality of the opposition. Passes still have to be made and held, kicks still have to be accurate, everyone still has to be mistake-free in their tasks and, perhaps the most difficult of all, the concentration still has to be total. It's far easier to lose concentration when you're seventy or eighty points up than it is if you're three points down with three minutes to play.

Lochore's rugby involvement and workload decreased considerably. He could concentrate on his farm again and spend more time with his family. He could do other things that had been put in abeyance and, perhaps most blessed of all, the phone rang less often.

Lochore and rugby can never be totally separated though. Casual visitors still showed up at the Lochore property, "Awatuna", to see him for themselves and to chat, sometimes to seek advice. Overseas reporters, whenever they were in the area, would never pass up the opportunity to call in for an interview.

There were occasional offers. Lochore spent a couple of weeks in Canada coaching in Edmonton and Toronto and found that enlightening, not having appreciated previously the enormous geographic, logistic and weather difficulties that Canadian rugby has to overcome. Rugby there is truly a minority sport and barely noticed in the shadow of sports such as ice hockey, baseball and football, and its adherents give new meaning to the word "enthusiasts".

At home, Lochore was brought onto an subcommittee set up by the New Zealand union to look at how the game could be developed. It was called the Game for the 90s committee and had some of the best rugby brains in the country, including Wilson Whineray, Ivan Vodanovich, John Hart, Laurie Mains, John Graham, Peter Goldsmith and Malcolm Dick. The chairman was Richie Guy, who had managed the World Cup All Blacks.

"That was a very enjoyable experience because we had a

235

range of people who understood rugby and who had a vision for its future and the clarity of thinking was amazing," Lochore says. "What we in effect did was produce a forerunner of the Boston Report and a lot of our ideas were later incorporated in that report. Some of the law changes we suggested were eventually adopted – such as the use it or lose it law that improved continuity – and some of the administrative methods we agreed would be ideal have come to pass.

"We should have been able to produce a blueprint for provincial rugby, but were told that was beyond our brief. We were adamant that a strong club and provincial base had to be retained and players needed to feel comfortable playing where they were based.

"We felt that rugby in some respects was being hindered by administrators being too concerned with the issues of the day instead of seeing the bigger picture or having a vision of the future. Too often administrators were putting a trampoline at the bottom of a cliff instead of seeing even a year or two beyond their present thinking. This has changed now and is still changing and we were very conscious at the time that if rugby was to change, it needed a new structure with administrators who could see beyond the immediate."

When the New Zealand union was planning its centenary season of 1992 and decided to have three official tests between the All Blacks and a World XV, Lochore's name was the first proposed for manager of the World team and there was no further discussion. It was an automatic and unanimous choice. There's something not quite right about someone of Lochore's stature in New Zealand rugby contributing to opposition to the All Blacks and when the World team beat the All Blacks in the first test, Lochore's emotions were mixed. It was a unique experience and an honour, and Lochore was pleased to be involved with rugby players of such diverse backgrounds – taking him back to his South African tour in 1979 – and coaches such as Ian McGeechan and Bob Templeton, both dedicated rugby men and long admirers of New Zealand rugby.

Such pleasurable tasks were short-term and not exactly onerous, and Lochore welcomed the opportunities to stay in touch with contemporary rugby, however briefly. He even played the unfamiliar role of spectator, going to Britain for the 1991 World Cup as just another supporter, though one more knowledgable than most.

"I didn't realise supporters on tour had so much fun," Lochore recalled. "It was a whole different way of appreciating rugby though from a purely New Zealand performance point of view, it wasn't that much fun. The All Blacks went much as I expected they would. I figured during their tour of Argentina in early 1991 that they would not be able to retain the World Cup. They weren't playing all that well and the selections, it seemed to me, were not based on form.

"The signs were there again when they just beat Australia in Auckland. By 1991, the All Blacks thought it was their right to win. They were using their skills but they weren't working hard enough and they did not deserve to win. The result of the semifinal in Dublin, when they were beaten by Australia, was justice. It showed you can't win a tournament like the World Cup by just thinking you're good enough. You've got to put in the hard work and the selectors have got to choose players at the right times and choose players who have put in the hard work. All Blacks should know there are no half measures, but they didn't seem to want to acknowledge that in 1991."

It was a different story in 1995 and by then Lochore was involved again. He'd had occasional conversations with the All Black coach, Laurie Mains, who had asked Lochore if he could help with the team's preparation on a casual basis. Lochore, of course, told Mains he would help whenever he could, but it became much more than casual.

Lochore's involvement in the World Cup came about because of the great standing he has in New Zealand rugby. It was as simple as that.

It was an involvement that had been considered and talked about long before the New Zealand union approved the campaign manager's role. Lochore, primarily because he had guided so successfully the 1987 campaign to win the first cup, had been invited onto a New Zealand union subcommittee whose brief was to plan the cup campaign. Laurie Mains and David Galvin, the union councillor who chaired the tours subcommittee and who was mainly responsible for the All Blacks' playing programme, knew that Lochore would be invaluable and saw that he was included.

Mains and Lochore had more in common than was publicly supposed. They were overlapping contemporaries as players and, in the freemasonry of rugby, they had known each other for about twenty years. They'd played All Black trials together – on the same day at Athletic Park in 1970, though in different matches – and had played a test together. The third against the British Isles in Wellington in 1971 was Mains' second test and the last for Lochore. They got to know each other even more as coaches, Lochore of New Zealand and Mains of Otago.

Lochore answered his country's call in 1971 and again in 1995. "I had a great deal of respect for Brian," Mains says, "first as a player and then as convenor of the All Black selectors when I was coaching Otago. I respected the way he dealt with provincial coaches and I recognised the mana he had in rugby, in New Zealand and around the world.

"I'd also been involved with him in the lead-up to the 1987 World Cup when he was convenor and coaching the All Blacks and I was called in to coach trial and zonal teams. He was a pleasure to work with and his knowledge of rugby and the respect people have for him was just immense."

As the build-up to 1995 began – and for Mains, it began in 1993 or even earlier, the cup was always in the back of the mind – Mains' thoughts turned increasingly to Lochore. He had already asked Lochore if he could call him for advice or just a chat from time to time and Lochore, of course, agreed. The need for a more formal role became increasingly evident. "I'd felt a bit frustrated at getting what I wanted from the New Zealand council," Mains recalls. "It wasn't that the council or the union were obstructive, it was more the time it took to get things and I felt that this time spent was detracting from my primary role. We had a manager, of course, but Colin Meads was busy with all the day-to-day detail and I don't think people generally realise just how much is involved in managing the All Blacks.

"I saw a need for a campaign manager with a dual role. One part would be to take the pressure off the manager and coach and the other to take care of organisational problems and who could best get responses from the New Zealand union for whatever was needed to win the cup. It was a liaison role, really, between us as the manager and coach and the New Zealand union in Wellington.

"When you're coaching a team, especially one as demanding as the All Blacks, the coach tends to get a bit of tunnel vision and what's needed is someone who recognises that and whose presence allows the coach to stay focused on his main job. Brian was ideal because he had been a great player, a successful coach and knew what was involved."

Initially, Rugby World Cup Ltd limitations on the size of tour parties decreed that a campaign manager was superfluous to requirements and that Lochore's role would have to end the moment the team took off for South Africa. "That would have been hard, waving goodbye to them from the airport," Lochore says. "I didn't expect from the outset that I would go to South Africa and I was happy to do what I could to help, but as we went from camp to camp and the squad took shape, the more I felt a part of it and the harder it would have been to say goodbye."

It became clear that the job would be incomplete if Lochore didn't go. The New Zealand union chairman, Eddie Tonks, talked to RWC and talked to the South African organisers and, eventually, the go-ahead for Lochore was given. It was the only possible decision. Lochore's input in New Zealand was critical to the eventual success of the campaign – and it was successful in all terms except the one that mattered, the winning of the cup. The All Blacks did everything but win it.

Would the All Blacks have played the way they did, stunned the rugby world the way they did, if Lochore hadn't been there? Mains says the answer to that question could never be known. "Perhaps we still could have," he says, "but the way we approached the cup and the way we played the games was part of the total package, in which Brian was an integral part. The way we played stemmed from the camps we'd had, right from the first in Queenstown. It's not an easy question to answer but I do know, and the players know, that Brian's presence was an immense help, in New Zealand and in South Africa."

The actual playing of the cup was still some time off when Lochore first became involved. His commission was a roving one, though he'd had a session in Wellington with Tonks and the union's chief executive officer, George Verry, to settle on some sort of definition. Detail wasn't easy, but the principle was not difficult. Lochore would help when and where he could, assist Meads and Mains in their missions with the sole aim of ensuring the All Blacks were prepared in the best possible way for the cup.

Among Lochore's first tasks was helping Mains with contracts. It was a new initiative for rugby. The idea was to sign the leading players till after the cup, guaranteeing their continued involvement and recompensing them for time spent in preparation. It was a sort of pre-dawn of the professional era that would soon be upon them, much sooner than anyone thought.

Lochore, Meads and Mains soon settled into a comfortable working team, compatibility evident – it couldn't have worked if it wasn't – and united in their aim. "We had a great understanding," Lochore says. "My role was never clearly defined and it had to be that way. Colin had lots of things to do and Laurie had to concentrate on the players and the playing, and I helped both of them and filled in the gaps. If Laurie wanted something from the New Zealand union, I would be the one to talk to Wellington. It was a liaison role in that respect and it all worked very well.

"It would be a mistake though to say that because the campaign manager role worked in 1995, we should have another one in 1999 or any other World Cup. It has to depend entirely on the circumstances and people of the time. I don't think a campaign manager can be foisted onto a manager and coach; that wouldn't work, just like giving a coach an assistant coach doesn't always work. It should be very much up to the people who are involved and, in 1995, we were fortunate that it worked very well."

Once in South Africa, the nature of the job changed. There was no New Zealand union to liaise with anymore and he found himself doing different chores, usually for whoever asked. He shouldered much of the news media burden – and it can be a burden at an event such as a World Cup when there are so many journalists with different requirements – and assisted Mains and Meads and the players whenever and wherever he could. "I was truly a jack of all trades," he laughed, modestly and inevitably but wrongly adding the second clause of the cliche, "and master of none."

Lochore was also involved early on, with Mains and Meads, in analysing players' fitness reports. As in 1987, they'd each been given tailored fitness programmes and were told in no uncertain terms that the programmes had to be carried out and standards met. If that didn't happen, they could forget about the World Cup.

At the training camp in Christchurch, this brought Jonah Lomu before the management. He'd been played in the two tests against France the year before and he'd been included in the cup training squad because of his obvious and enormous potential. But potential alone would not get him to the World Cup. He had to do the work like everyone else and, in Christchurch, it was evident that he had not been doing the work. Neither had lock Mark Cooksley.

241

"We talked to them individually in Christchurch and told them they had a month. If their fitness was not what we wanted by then, their contracts would be terminated. They'd been given all the assistance possible by people such as Martin Toomey, the fitness adviser. As it turned out, Jonah improved and Mark didn't. Jonah realised what it meant, that being an All Black was not just a matter of being big and fast and having potential. He learned that he had to work to be an All Black, just like everyone else."

Lochore recalls the Lomu improvement as dramatic, an improvement not just in fitness but also in attitude and commitment. Lomu was transformed, as a direct result of the blunt talk in Christchurch, from being a big footballer of potential to an All Black of a status previously totally unknown in any New Zealand sport, or in any New Zealand walk of life. His deeds in South Africa were still to come but when the new Lomu reappeared in front of Lochore, the signs were plain to see.

"Jonah was in a New Zealand XV to play Canada in Palmerston North the day before the other All Blacks played as the Harlequins in Hamilton against Waikato. Eric Rush was in the Harlequins team but was injured so we called Jonah up from Palmerston North.

"I will never forget him at training in Hamilton. He was immense. I have never seen anything like it. He did everything at super pace with super power. He hit Paul Henderson once and Ginge, who's no softy, bounced back ten metres and landed on his backside. He hit Richard Loe, and everyone knows how hard he is, and he bounced back ten metres. We couldn't believe what we were watching. From then on, there was no way he was not going to the World Cup."

Just to emphasise the point he'd already made, Lomu scored three tries against Waikato, each of them using his immense power and speed. A phenomenon had not been born, he'd been made by the harsh lesson he'd had: get fit or get out.

The All Blacks slipped into South Africa the way Lochore wanted: quietly and without fuss or fanfare. They were in Johannesburg, but the focus was on the other end of the country, in Cape Town, where the welcoming functions were held and where South Africa played their first World Cup match against the 1991 winners, Australia. The All Blacks were able to get on with their training and preparations for their first match, against Ireland, with the minimum of publicity and it helped that England were in a different pool and were down in Durban, keeping the insatiable British press away from the All Blacks.

The opening days of the campaign went smoothly, but not so smoothly as to induce complacency – management and players were always conscious that improvement was still needed. "We were still making enough errors to give us something to build on," Lochore said. "The first two games, Ireland and Wales, were both at night and we're not great players at night. We're not good at sitting around all day and the different routine of night matches can be upsetting. The lights in Johannesburg were good, but still not daylight, it's just not the same."

The All Blacks had shown enough in those two games to make others sit up and take notice. There was the Lomu factor, of course. But there was more than that. There was an added speed and urgency to the All Black game, an expansiveness that had not been there in recent years. It was no accident. Lochore, Mains and Meads and others had plotted the playing method months before, starting with the camp in Queenstown when Lochore had told them of the 1987 campaign and how the All Blacks had to have superior speed of thought and action to overcome height and weight deficiencies. It was the style of play that had been the hallmark of the national provincial championship in recent years, particularly but not exclusively by Otago, and it was the style of play that could win the World Cup.

Japan were next and since New Zealand had already qualified for the quarterfinals, the match in Bloemfontein gave Mains the opportunity he wanted to select those who had not so far had a game. This included one of his most important players, lock Robin Brooke, who had been injured and hence reacquainted with the nickname of "Food Bill" that he'd acquired on the 1993 tour of England and Scotland when he did not play a game.

"Japan was one of the highlights of the World Cup," Lochore said. "It was as close to perfect rugby as I've seen. I can't recall a single mistake in the first half and that's amazing when you consider the pace at which the game was played and that several of the players had not played for three or more weeks."

The World Cup finals record score of 145-17 naturally enough brought out the knockers and the cynics who derided the game as a mismatch and saw the scoreline as being as meaningless as a Harlem Globetrotters winning sequence.

Lochore bridles at such suggestions. "Try and score 140 points against anyone, the players know how difficult it is and what's required. The discipline and concentration levels have to be even sharper than they would be for a supposedly harder opponent. Other than the England game, that match in Bloemfontein was the highlight for me. I was especially pleased for the fellows who weren't getting the other games, people like Paul Henderson and Simon Culhane and Marc Ellis and others, who did the job so well, and it was a great launching pad for the two Brookes, especially Robin. The game came at the right time too, allowing us a mental break from being in Johannesburg all the time."

In the days between the Japan match and the quarterfinal against Scotland, Lochore had to do something he hates doing and, when he does do it, doesn't do it very well: tell lies – or, if not actually tell lies, at least not tell the whole truth. It became one of Lochore's less happy memories of the World Cup.

It was not exactly a world-shattering issue. The All Blacks had always planned a bit of rest and recreation in a game park north of Pretoria after Japan. It was part of the fine detail the All Black management had worked out during the preparation months in New Zealand.

What hadn't been in the plan was the method of transport to the game park. Commercial flights had been scheduled but some high-powered strings were pulled by someone and the All Blacks in Pretoria were packed into military transport aircraft. While en route to an air force base near the game park, the All Blacks were treated to the spectacle of the aircraft flying in formation and refuelling a flight of fighters in mid-air. It may be an everyday occurrence to pilots, but it was a unique experience to rugby players whose feet are normally firmly on the ground. The South African Air Force completed its hospitality programme by flying the All Blacks from the base to the game park in a couple of transport helicopters.

"This was all done on the quiet and we were asked not to talk about it because there was a fear that the word would get about that the All Blacks were getting preferential treatment and every team would want the same privilege," Lochore said. "So when we were back in Pretoria and had a press conference, I had to deceive the press and I found it very hard. It's very difficult to tell lies. We talked about the game park and that was easy enough because it was spectacular and we all enjoyed it thoroughly, but then the reporters asked how we got there. 'Ah, we flew,' I said. 'What in?' 'Ah, an aeroplane.' 'What sort?' 'Oh I don't know, just an aeroplane like any other.' It was very difficult misleading them like this. I've always been upfront with the press and I found this experience very hard."

The All Blacks for the second time in a World Cup quarterfinal played Scotland and for the second time beat them comprehensively, though Lochore remembered Scotland in 1987 as being a better team than in 1995. "They played as well as they had done in recent years. From our point of view, it was a good game because we made enough mistakes to keep us working hard and to keep us sharp for the semifinal. We were never in danger of being beaten but we let them score more points than we should have."

The semifinal against England, once England had accounted

for Australia, was uppermost in the management minds but not talked about among the players till Scotland were disposed of. To look forward more than the immediate game can be fatal in such a high-level tournament; can be disastrous at any time.

England were the team the All Blacks wanted to beat most. They were delighted they were playing England and not Australia. The 1993 loss to England at Twickenham, and it was a case of the All Blacks losing rather than England winning, stuck in the players' craw.

"A lot of the players were still smarting after the 1993 result," Lochore said. "We don't like being beaten by them. I don't suppose anyone does. There was a lot more feeling going into the England game in Cape Town than there would have been for a semifinal against anyone else. It was more than a semifinal. We had a point to prove and we wanted to prove it in the most emphatic way.

"It was absolutely vital that we knew how we were going to play it. We talked about it, we planned it, we knew precisely what we would do at any given moment or in any given circumstance. There was never any doubt about how we would play it, just doubts about whether the tactics would come off. The amazing thing was how completely they did work. Everything we planned, we did. Everything we talked about, happened. Everything we thought England might do, they did. The key to the game was speed, speed of thought and action, getting the ball wide, getting it to Jonah, and running at them. It all succeeded beyond our wildest dreams."

Supporters draped in flags of St George and with red and white painted faces and English accents thronged the streets of Cape Town and crammed into Newlands. When the All Blacks made their customary pre-match ground inspection, all they could hear was English singing, English cheers. *Swing Low Sweet Chariot* was not No 1 on the New Zealand hit parade. When they ran out onto the field, again it was the English supporters who dominated. It took only a couple of minutes for the English voices to fall still and for New Zealand accents to rend the air.

"We didn't take much notice of the other semifinal that was played the day before because we didn't want it to detract from our concentration and focus. But we knew playing the home team in the final would be much more difficult than playing anyone else. South Africa might have been lucky to get into the final and the French unlucky but we couldn't be bothered with that. South Africa were there and we were to play them at Ellis Park in front of a capacity crowd, most of them yelling themselves hoarse for South Africa. But we knew we could do it. Everything had gone according to plan so far."

The All Blacks flew back to Pretoria from Cape Town the night of the semifinal. They didn't want to wait around longer than they had to and Cape Town was awash with England supporters and the All Blacks did not want to mix with them. Many of them had spent the night before the semifinal singing outside the All Blacks' hotel.

There was a nicely ironic touch at Cape Town airport. The All Blacks arrived for their flight and went to wait in the business class lounge, but found the England players had got there first. Not wishing to disturb them, they were taken straight onto the aircraft and ushered into the first class compartment, despite not having tickets for it. It was satisfying a few minutes later when the England players boarded the same aircraft and were ushered past the All Blacks, in their stretched-out opulence, down to cattle class. "It was a perfect ending to a perfect day," Lochore said, though he wondered who would have sat where if the result of the match at Newlands had gone the other way.

The All Blacks had a night at the Pretoria hotel in which they had stayed for the Scotland quarterfinal, then moved to their Johannesburg hotel on the Monday. The serious planning began. There was one match left. The most important match. For many of the players, the most important match they would ever play. For Laurie Mains, the most important match in which he would coach the All Blacks. It was the match that signalled the end of the road. The planning as much as the playing would determine whether it was a high road or a low road.

Towards the end of 1994, which had not been a very satisfying season with losses to France and two fortuitous wins and a draw against South Africa, Laurie Mains made the astounding comment to a rugby writer that the All Blacks had been holding something back for the World Cup. The writer reported Mains' views without comment, but others were stunned. All Blacks holding something back in a test? Surely not. No All Black worth his jersey would do such a thing. A test match is a test match to be won. Forget the future. Win for the moment.

Lochore confirmed that what Mains said was accurate, but not in the sense it was picked up. It was not a case of the All Blacks not trying in the 1994 tests, it was more a matter of not revealing some ploys until the World Cup. Tactics had been devised for the World Cup and it would have been imprudent to have revealed them the year before when opponents, and especially Australia and South Africa, would have had a few months to work out counters. It made the All Blacks' impact in 1995 so much greater.

South Africans were genuinely stunned by the way the All Blacks played there. They were worried. The World Cup, awarded to them in 1992 when South Africa was in the chrysalis stage of its emergence from apartheid, was now the international stage on which South Africa would show the world it was one people, one nation, the rainbow nation as Nelson Mandela fondly called it. Mandela himself bore the message to the world by his appearance in the Springboks' dressing room before the first match in Cape Town and by his public and warm endorsement of the Springboks, formerly the symbol of white supremacy. For the metamorphosis to be complete, according to the South African script, the Springboks had to win.

The All Blacks at the beginning of the week in Johannesburg

248

knew this and they knew that the final had acquired a status of being more than just a rugby match, however important and significant in itself. They also knew the only way to overcome this would be utter and total concentration on their own planning and their own game.

On the Monday, there was a meeting of all the team management plus the captain, Sean Fitzpatrick, and centre Frank Bunce. It was a strategy meeting for the week. "Several of us had been there as players and we discussed how desperate they would be to win and what a win would mean to them," Lochore said. "We looked at all the possibilities of what might happen during the week. We thought they may try to discredit us in the press but they could only do that by dredging up old stuff. We'd been squeaky clean. We talked about it with the players and thought if they tried it, it would have the opposite effect and just make us closer."

The planning was so detailed and thorough, they even talked about food, uncannily anticipating events that were tragically soon to unfold.

"We knew the All Blacks had a problem with food in Sydney in 1980 and we discussed that. We decided we should all eat in the main dining room and not get isolated. Players would not go out in twos and threes to restaurants in the area. What they ate would be pre-determined and supervised."

The Australians had had the use of a personal chef while they were based in Cape Town and when the All Blacks were there for the semifinal against England, they used his services too. "It was the best food we had the whole time we were there," Mains recalled. The All Blacks decided to seek his services in Johannesburg now they were no longer required by the homeward bound Wallabies.

Discussions continued, decisions were made. The meeting broke up and each man went off to fulfil his allotted tasks. Lochore, other things crowding in on his mind as F-Day approached, thought little more about it. He bumped into the team doctor, Mike Bowen, in the diningroom doorway one morning and asked him about the chef. "How's he working out?"

"He wasn't able to come," Bowen replied.

Lochore felt a shudder of apprehension, even premonition.

Mains said the management at the team's hotel in Johannesburg had been obstructive, unwilling to allow an outside chef to cook for the hotel's most important guests. In Cape Town, he had had the sole use of a spare kitchen and was able to work independently of the hotel kitchen staff. To do that in Johannesburg was, apparently, not possible.

Thursday lunchtime was spent, as normal, in the team's separate dining room in the hotel. On the menu that day were hamburgers, chickenburgers, lasagne, sandwiches, fruit juice, milk, tea and coffee.

On the Thursday night, tension crowding in on the whole party, Lochore and Meads decided it would be appropriate to do something for the non-players, those party members traditionally known in rugby as "dirty dirties". All the management team, but not Mike Bowen, were included in this normally most pleasurable of tasks.

They went out to a restaurant and had a pleasant time but there was an edge in the air. The final was too close for any to truly relax. The dinner party broke up about ten o'clock and the managers and players bussed back to the hotel. Lochore was with Meads and Mains. "On the way back, Colin and Laurie complained a bit about stomach pains and I thought it must have been something we ate in the restaurant. I was fine and I thought it was just a temporary thing."

When they arrived back at their hotel, the bottom of Lochore's world fell out. The bottom of Mains' world fell out. The bottom of Meads' world fell out. Waiting anxiously for them in the lobby of the hotel was Zinzan Brooke. He's normally relaxed, affable, a smile never far away. This night he was tense and worried. As soon as Lochore saw him, he knew something was terribly wrong.

"The boys are crook," Brooke blurted. "They're spewing up all over the place."

Devastated, the management team with Bowen leading the way made a hurried round of all the players' rooms. Brooke had not been exaggerating. Bowen did what he could, but the damage had been done. Some of the players were dreadfully ill; most felt, at best, queasy.

"Colin had a shocking night," Lochore said. "He got up during the night and collapsed and had to get the doctor. He was in a shocking state. He and Jeff Wilson couldn't get out of their beds on the Friday. Others should have been in bed. Of the final players, Jeff Wilson and Andrew Mehrtens were the worst affected.

"With Colin in bed and clearly not well, I virtually took over as manager. I talked to Laurie and Colin and we decided to keep it quiet, to keep it within the team. We didn't want a word of it leaking out, we didn't want the South Africans to think they had any physical or psychological advantage over us. When it did get out later, it sounded like sour grapes and that was unfortunate because it certainly wasn't intended that way.

"We went to Ellis Park in the morning for a private run that was more of a walk. Because it was private, there were no pressmen there so it was relatively easy to keep it quiet. I suppose it helped too that it was the day the southern hemisphere countries announced their television deal with Rupert Murdoch so that kept the pressmen busy.

"All the players except for Wilson went to Ellis Park, though many of them were suffering. If the final had been on the Friday, we would have struggled to get 15 players onto the field. I took the dirties down one end of the ground and Laurie took the team down the other and we told them the whole 26 would have to be ready to play the next day because we didn't know who would be well enough and who wouldn't.

"In the afternoon, instead of sitting around in hotel rooms worrying and wondering, we took them to a nearby park, just for a wander around in the fresh air. Some didn't wander at all, just slumped down and leaned against the nearest tree. It was a tragedy."

The final was already lost. The rest of the world didn't know it, but Lochore, in his heart, knew it. He knew that everything had been perfect – New Zealand had 26 fit players to pick from – until then. It had gone exactly as it had in 1987 and he had no doubts, no doubts at all, that the All Blacks would have won the final.

The night before the final, all the players attended team meetings and all stayed in the hotel. The night before a match is usually the night out for the dirty dirties, but they couldn't go because they knew they may be called upon. The night out has become a tradition on tours and it's assumed the position of being a superstition, a part of the routine that dare not be stopped. So as not to break the spell, Mike Bowen, Earle Kirton, media man Ric Salizzo and others had the night out for the dirty dirties. Their hearts were not in it.

The players' conditions were better on the Saturday morning but Wilson and Mehrtens were still ailing. Others were and didn't say. Meads looked as if he'd seen a ghost.

To the New Zealanders at Ellis Park, to those at home watching in the wee hours of the morning on television, to New Zealanders around the world watching wherever they could, the All Blacks looked tense when they lined up, but that was only to be expected before a World Cup final. Wilson looked pale, but his complexion is fair anyway. Mehrtens too. The handshakes with Nelson Mandela were cursory, the hands doing what a tiny part of the brain bid them but the players' thoughts far away from the symbol of South African unity before them.

Lochore, Mains, Meads and Kirton were up in the stand, their hearts heavy. They felt desperately for the players. They hoped they might still win, but knew they could not, not against such a background and not against a Springbok team that knew it was playing for the first time for all of South Africa.

Once the game began, astute New Zealand observers could see that all was not well. The urgency wasn't the same, the confidence was lacking, the edge had gone off. The spirit was still there, for some the spirit that got them out of sick beds and onto the field.

The longer the game wore on, a game of attrition, a game of waiting for mistakes amid indescribable tension, the more evident it was that these All Blacks were not the All Blacks who had played at Cape Town the Sunday before. Hearts beating beneath New Zealand blazers in the stand swelled with pride the way the All Blacks still tried, still forced extra time and didn't give up till the last.

Food poisoning was blamed; some said it was deliberate. There was even a theory that somehow involved British bookmakers. Once reporters found out about it after the final, chefs, waiters and managers were interviewed, but with no firm conclusions.

Lochore does not subscribe to theories. To do so would be pointless. It happened. The final was lost. Yet again, All Blacks were denied in South Africa – painfully, agonisingly.

"I have no idea whether it was a mistake or an accident or whatever," he says. "All I know is that it happened."

11

A GAME IN CRISIS

If not winning the World Cup final had struck a blow to the core of New Zealand rugby, there was worse to come. Much worse. It is not over-stating the severity to say that the events that unfolded in the weeks after the cup threatened the very existence of New Zealand rugby, put in jeopardy a century of tradition and generations of pride.

New Zealand rugby was faced with the very real prospect of having no All Blacks. It had had a multi-million dollar promise from news media magnate Rupert Murdoch in return for television rights for ten years, but no-one at the centre of the crisis kidded themselves about that. They knew if New Zealand rugby did not have All Blacks, neither would it have Murdoch's money.

Not only were All Blacks in danger of going elsewhere, so were leading provincial players who would have been the obvious replacements. Rugby would have been left with a base and a shell.

Lochore knew nothing of this in South Africa. On the Saturday night of the final, he'd gone to the farewell dinner with the players and was as annoyed and insulted by South African Rugby Union president Louis Luyt's speech as all other New Zealanders in the room. It was a gross insensitivity from a man not often known for his tact.

"We boasted in '87 that the real World Cup was not won by New Zealand because we were not there," Luyt said. "Then in '91, we boasted again. We were not there. Then in '95, we proved that if we had been there, we would have won." The World Cup, he told the hundreds at the dinner, was now in its rightful home. If that wasn't enough to make the blood boil, Luyt then made his infamous presentation of a gold watch to Welsh referee Derek Bevan, who had refereed the Springboks' first match, against Australia, and their close-run semifinal against France. The watch was later returned.

The All Blacks quietly walked out. Lochore and Colin Meads agreed it was the thing to do and, when they got outside the dining room, they found the English and French players and the referees were already there, obviously as incensed with Luyt as the New Zealanders had been.

"Mike Brewer and Paul Henderson said something to Luyt but I had no contact with him," Lochore said. "I was disappointed with what he'd said. I've known him a long time, he was very helpful to us in 1970 when he wasn't involved with the South African union. I regard him as a personal friend. During the World Cup, he hadn't been obstructive in any way – in fact very helpful. He's a very generous man but there are two sides to him."

The next day, the All Blacks had a final team session. "We were devastated," Lochore said. "Not because we were denied victory, but because we thought we had let New Zealand down. We didn't want to take the gloss off the win for South Africa, it was fair and well done. They won, we lost. No excuses."

On the Monday, the day before departure, Lochore and Sean Fitzpatrick had a round of golf, during which, significantly, neither money nor the future shape of rugby was discussed.

There had been some talk in South Africa, though Lochore had not been privy to it. Richie Guy, the New Zealand union chairman, had wanted to explain the Murdoch deal to the players before the final but the All Black management wouldn't allow it – it would be too distracting, especially given that the All Blacks already had problems on their minds. Guy instead spoke to them on the Saturday night before the dinner, briefly outlining the agreement that had been reached and said the future of New Zealand rugby was bright and he would talk to them more after they were home. No-one then mentioned to Guy or to Lochore that there was more than Murdoch's money in the offing, that a plan had been hatched in the name of a former Australian test player and administrator, Ross Turnbull, to form a "world championship" under the aegis of the registered company World Rugby Corporation. Creaming off the top players from many countries, predominantly New Zealand, Australia and South Africa – the very three who had stitched together the deal with News Corporation – a series of international matches would be played, sometimes in exotic, in a rugby sense, locales such as Kuala Lumpur and Hong Kong. Allied with Turnbull were two Sydney lawyers, Michael Hill and Jeff Levy.

It was to dominate their lives for weeks. Lochore recalled that he first heard of it in much the same manner as most New Zealanders, by speculative stories in newspapers or on radio.

None of the players he had guided through the World Cup campaign took him into their confidence and Lochore was left, like the rugby union and the public, trying to sift fact from rumours, truth from lies and forthrightness from deceit.

Guy's explanation to the All Blacks of what was planned under the Murdoch deal was, of necessity, brief because it was between the final and the farewell dinner, not an ideal time to unfold plans that would in all likelihood affect the financial futures of all involved. It was arranged to meet again about a week after the return home when the All Black party was in Wellington for a parliamentary reception.

Amid the finger food and the politicians' jollity at mixing with the famous, few knew what was about to unfold. Of those who did, none were saying.

The All Blacks and management after the reception went to the rugby union headquarters at the Huddart Parker building in central Wellington for Guy's briefing.

"Richie had talked for a while and the players asked if they could be left on their own for a while," Lochore recalled. "I got the distinct impression that Richie hadn't finished his presentation. I understood that we would be rejoining the players after they'd had their chat but they had left the NZRFU offices without saying a word, without further contact or explanation. Richie had already asked me in South Africa if I would act on behalf of the union in contracting the players. I'd agreed reluctantly and he'd told the players that night of my role. Clearly, the meeting after the parliamentary reception was inconclusive and we needed another meeting soon.

"The contracts had not been completed and the players in Wellington I thought were a little unfair on Richie. It wasn't a high-grade presentation, but it was interrupted before he was finished."

Lochore had agreed to help the union because it seemed a fairly simple operation. "I wouldn't have agreed if I'd known what was to develop."

On the following Sunday, a fortnight before the first Bledisloe Cup test in Auckland, the two sides met again. Representing the union were Guy, Lochore, All Black manager Colin Meads, coach Laurie Mains and Jock Hobbs, the former captain under Lochore and a recently elected union councillor whose role over the next few weeks was to be critical. For the players, there were Sean Fitzpatrick, Ian Jones and Eric Rush. Rush is a lawyer.

"The meeting was very amicable and we went through aspects of the contracts and the players seemed happy enough with the meeting," Lochore said. "We wanted to get it done and finished with because we'd heard that some players had league offers, but the players said they did not want to be sidetracked with contract negotiations in the time leading up to the two tests against Australia.

"I readily agreed with that view, but clearly there was a concern about league offers to some players. Rush agreed and said he knew of three players approached by league clubs and that they may want to talk to me. I said I'd be only too happy to talk to them anytime and he said he'd ring them and let them know. I never heard from any of them."

Neither Turnbull nor WRC were mentioned at that meeting.

Rumours circulated rapidly, as they tend to do, and were positively racing around the country as the week of the first test against Australia neared. The news media speculated; it could only speculate because no-one who knew what was going on would say. Lochore, Guy, Hobbs and the rest of the union were in much the same position as the reporters – they had heard stories but confirmation was difficult if not impossible to obtain.

"Clearly, there was now another issue," Lochore says, "and it had to be dealt with quickly. The New Zealand union council met in Auckland on the morning of the test and Rob Fisher [the union's deputy chairman], Jock and I were formed into a subcommittee to negotiate contracts with the players."

A meeting was arranged with the whole All Black squad at their Auckland headquarters, the Poenamo on the North Shore, the day after the Australians were beaten at Eden Park. Lawyers Bernie Allen and Deryck Dallow from the Auckland law firm Davenports were there, representing the players.

"It was a strange meeting. We were upfront with what we could offer and what we thought, but they didn't tell us much. They told us absolutely nothing about WRC. They were obviously aware of what was going on, but chose not to tell us. Our job was to talk about how important it was for them to remain loyal to New Zealand rugby and we reiterated that we would stick to the players' wish not to negotiate contracts until after the Bledisloe Cup matches."

While Lochore and the union were sticking to their word and giving the players the distraction-free time they wanted to prepare to play Australia in the second match, it became abundantly clear that the players had no such qualms negotiating with WRC.

More information leaked in the week between the two Bledisloe Cup tests. Lochore had been intending to fly from Wellington to Sydney on the afternoon before the second test but at about eleven o'clock on the Thursday night received a phone call from Hobbs, who was already in Sydney, advising him to get across the Tasman as quick as he could.

It is not easy, when you're a farmer in the Wairarapa without your own Learjet, to answer such a summons. Lochore spent the next couple of hours on the phone and eventually was able to book on an early-morning flight out of Wellington. By the time he'd packed for the weekend and taking into account the two-hour driving time to the airport, there was precious little time left to sleep.

Lochore, Fisher and Hobbs, joined by another union councillor, Richard Crawshaw, spent the Friday in a lawyer's office in Sydney, going over the contracts they would offer the All Blacks almost as soon as referee Brian Stirling from Ireland blew the whistle for the last time. They prepared letters of intent and contracts for the All Blacks well into the night and presented these to a specially convened meeting of the New Zealand union council the next morning. It was the first time the council had met outside New Zealand.

"The situation was desperate and we needed wide powers to retrieve the situation," Lochore said. "We gave the council a rundown on what we had done the previous week and they agreed with what we suggested."

That same morning, back in Wellington, *The Dominion* made public for the first time the true extent of WRC's involvement with the All Blacks. It said that 23 of the 26 World Cup All Blacks had signed with Turnbull by a deadline of the previous Thursday night – the night Lochore got his late-night summons from Hobbs. It reported they were expecting to be paid more than $US500,000 over three years, with a down-payment in November of about $100,000.

The players who had said they did not want to negotiate with the rugby union for fear it would interfere with their match preparation had instead been secretly negotiating with a body that was directly opposed to the union.

The Bledisloe Cup match in Sydney should have been a celebration. It was the 100th test between the two countries and the Australian union had invited former players from both sides to be introduced to the Sydney Football Stadium crowd before the match and to a lavish centenary dinner afterwards. The past was worth celebrating, and so was the present because the All Blacks won 34-23, but the future was uncertain.

"There was a lot of discussion at the dinner among the older All Blacks," Lochore said, though he took no part. "It was neither the time nor the place for that sort of thing, but I know some of the old players were pretty angry about what was going on. There were some, how shall we say it, interesting conversations that night. I stayed out of it as best I could but I did hear John Ashworth saying he wanted his son to be able to play for the All Blacks. That was the sort of feeling there was.

"Straight after the match I delivered to the All Blacks' dressing room the letters of intent Jock, Rob, Richard and myself had been working on throughout the previous day and night. Colin Meads handed them out. Jock and Rob missed seeing the match live to make sure everything was completed correctly. It was very important to get it right at that time."

After the match and before the dinner, the All Blacks went off somewhere by bus for their own meeting. What was discussed was not divulged to Lochore or other union people.

The extent of the WRC incursion into rugby was by now quite plain and New Zealand union councillors and Lochore knew that if the All Blacks went, the News Corporation money would in all probability be withdrawn. Sam Chisholm, the News Corp executive who had been most involved in the deal, naturally enough thought when he bought the television rights that the best players from the three countries would be playing. He would not have agreed if he'd known he was buying rights to games involving second or third best.

The potential loss of the money was alarming enough. Even more alarming, especially to someone such as Lochore who was the epitome of what All Black rugby meant to New Zealand, was the potential loss of the All Blacks. This was what alarmed the older players in Sydney and this was what alarmed people throughout New Zealand.

Back in New Zealand, the hastily formed negotiating teams started talking to groups of players, trying to persuade them that their future and rugby's future lay with loyalty to the New Zealand union, a loyalty that would now – for the first time – be handsomely financially rewarded.

"I came home on the Sunday and on the Monday flew to Auckland to begin the round of meeting players on their own patches," Lochore said. "I started with Auckland, North Harbour and Counties, then Waikato, Wellington and Bay of Plenty. My team comprised myself, Tony Ward from the rugby union staff in Wellington and lawyers Sarah Sinclair and Penny Freeman. We confronted the players and put our case. Jock was doing a similar job in the South Island and the lower part of the North.

"There was a full attendance at the Auckland meeting but the North Harbour meeting was strange. Only eight or nine players showed up. I know Ian Jones was there and I know Eric Rush wasn't. What was strange was that the North Harbour management was so negative toward the union's proposal and contracts and seeming to see no good in anything that was suggested."

Among the myriad of rumours at the time was one that Laurie Mains was also involved with WRC, which would have been an untenable position for the All Black coach and, as such, a servant of the union. Lochore, who had heard the rumour, was due to speak at the Otago Sportsman of the Year dinner and, before going south, he phoned Mains and told him he'd like to see him. The two met and Lochore asked Mains the direct question: are you involved? Mains assured Lochore he was not. Lochore accepted the assurance.

Hobbs bore the brunt of the endless round of negotiations, meetings with players and lawyers and constant phone calls and

Lochore was appalled when, a few months later, delegates to the New Zealand union special general meeting could find no room for Hobbs on the reconstituted board that replaced the rugby union council.

Lochore is no lover of the old, parochial and selfish methods that historically rule when provincial delegates meet to vote, relying on the discredited philosophy of "you scratch my back and I'll scratch yours".

"Rugby will continue to suffer if people vote with their feet instead of their hearts and heads," he said. "Because Jock was so straight and so thorough and uncompromising in the tasks he'd been given, it cost him his position. Delegates have to learn that mistakes like this will not be tolerated in the future; we must get the right people, people like Jock." It was a sad irony that Lochore was later a member of the appointments committee that decided on the two independent members of the board. Hobbs, not wishing to attempt a circuitous route onto the board, was not among the applicants.

The efficacy of the Lochore and Hobbs teams became apparent within the first week after the test in Australia, and perhaps their impact was so great the players started to feel beleaguered, as if they'd lost public support. They made a curious public statement on a Saturday to Sunday newspapers in an effort to regain some ground. No name was put to it and no All Black has since claimed authorship. In terms of news media management, it was a public relations disaster. Even the greenest of politicians knows that public statements on a Saturday are a waste of time.

Its positioning in the *Sunday Star-Times* didn't help the players' cause either. It was down the bottom of a page and above it was the weekly column by another one time All Black captain, David Kirk. "I am confident that the game will survive the current threat," Kirk wrote. "First, I think the national unions, not the international entrepreneurs, will win and second, even if they don't and the top 25 or so players in New Zealand are lost, they will be the losers. "The selfishness of a few will not dim the light of those who are prepared to give to the spirit of rugby rather than from the trough of financial gain."

Much of what the All Blacks – or some of the All Blacks, since no names were attached – said in their statement defied credibility, especially once the third sentence was reached: "And we want to assure them [the rugby public] that at all times the traditions, the culture and the future viability of the game are paramount in our thinking."

Rather, it was men such as Lochore and Hobbs who were giving paramountcy to such values.

The threat to the game slowly receded as the work put in by Hobbs and Lochore paid dividends and as some Australian and South African players were also being wooed back from the brink.

The breakthrough came in New Zealand on August 10 from Otago, when Hobbs announced the signings of two high-profile players, Jeff Wilson and Josh Kronfeld, and several others from Otago and other provinces. On the same day, the Australian union announced it was taking a different route and starting negotiations with WRC.

"Once the Otago breakthrough came and the negotiations were more about legal aspects, I became less involved," Lochore said. "That pretty much ended my involvement though I was in constant phone contact with Jock, sometimes two or three times a day. It was amazing how long it went on; it was about October before the last were signed.

"I don't think the New Zealand public ever really appreciated, even now, just what a threat to rugby the WRC had been. Everyone knew the All Blacks had been targeted, and most had agreed, but what a lot of people didn't realise was that WRC was after the top 150 or so players and, if it had gone ahead, the New Zealand union would have had to start again with nothing.

"In the end, it wasn't just a matter of money. We had to argue that their continuing was vital for the good of New Zealand rugby. I know the public thought the All Blacks were just being greedy, but a lot of them in the end took less money in their rugby union contracts than they were being promised by WRC or Super League and I applaud that, though at the time we'd been given no 'official' figures of what WRC was actually promising. It was all speculation."

Twenty of the World Cup All Blacks committed themselves, in the end, to the rugby union. Those who didn't were Marc Ellis (who went to the Auckland Warriors), Graeme Bachop (returned to Japan), Ant Strachan (Japan), Mike Brewer (retired and went to work in Ireland), Jamie Joseph (Japan) and Kevin Schuler (Japan).

During the whole saga, Lochore had no individual contact with any of the players, even though he'd been so close to them in the immediately preceding months. "I can understand the position some of them were in and how they were under a great deal of pressure, but I was disappointed and a little hurt that the players obviously felt they wouldn't be comfortable talking to me. I was disappointed they appeared to assume that I wouldn't be able to see it from their point of view."

Lochore was able to sit back and smile months later when rugby league's battle between the Australian Rugby League and Murdoch's Super League – the catalyst for rugby going to Murdoch in the first place – broke down into internecine legal warfare. "The players were saying they were doing what was best for the game and it wasn't just a matter of money – we'd been through all that. What happened in league was an exact replica of what had happened in rugby. Fortunately, we had the players and the administrators with loyalty and tradition in rugby to make the difference and reach a satisfactory outcome."

The writing of history can never be as risky, dramatic and traumatic as living it, and Lochore is conscious that whatever and however many words are eventually written about what happened in 1995, they will never do full justice to the work put in by those, especially Jock Hobbs, who literally saved the game.

Lochore was also thankful it happened the way it did, which may sound a curious way of putting it. "I was happy with what we achieved in a short time, there were an incredible number of far-reaching decisions. I think maybe in ten years we'll look back and think, 'Thank goodness it happened that way.' If we'd had more time, there would have been more pontificating, more subcommittees would have been formed and Jock and whoever wouldn't have been given the powers and the rein that we had. But the decisions had to be made then and they were."

It had been the most tumultuous year in the game's history – more significant than anything that had gone before, much more historic than any of the South African arguments that New Zealand had to endure and much more meaningful than the split a century before that led to the formation of league.

A direct result of the negotiations in New Zealand, Australia and South Africa was that the International Rugby Board at meetings in Paris and Tokyo was presented with a fait accompli: declare the game professional. It did so, and the move was welcomed by Lochore as one that had been inevitable for years. It made its declaration unconditional and that's where Lochore has doubts.

"The game at the highest level had no option but to be professional and, let's face it, we'd been professional in everything but amounts paid for several years. Professionalism is more than just about money, it's also attitude and preparation and a host of other things.

"The worry was in the IRB saying the whole game is professional. I'm very concerned that professionalism could go too far down the ranks. It could put enormous pressure on clubs, which are the very bedrock of the game in New Zealand and one of the reasons why New Zealand rugby has been so consistently strong."

Lochore is also worried about the "market forces" of professionalism that see some players getting huge amounts and others, by comparison, not much. "I know it's a naive view, but, in an ideal world, all the top rugby players would get the same amount of money because it's a total team game and one can't exist without the other. But it's not an ideal world and I know that there is such a thing as market value and that some players can generate more income than others.

"Guys I feel sorry for are people like Ian Jones, who's done an enormous amount for New Zealand rugby. He's there, match in and match out, winning ball for us and doing everything required of him, yet he is not of the same market value as some other players."

The sum of the various changes had immediate effect early in 1996 with the beginning of the Super 12. "That's a marvellous concept and a vast improvement on the Super 10 or its other predecessors. What they did was cut out the majority of the country. Any area of New Zealand that didn't have teams couldn't have cared less about the Super 10 and even those that were in it sometimes didn't seem to care, as if it was a warm-up pre-season exercise.

"The way the Super 12 structure is now involves everyone and it gives a chance for players from second or third division unions to play at a level they otherwise wouldn't play at. My greatest note of caution is that the drafted players must return to their home provinces for the NPC. That's the whole point of it. It would be disastrous if some drafted players decided they liked being wherever they were drafted to and they were allowed to stay there, or if they were invited to stay. It's one of the reasons why I'm against provincial coaches also coaching Super 12 teams because, with all the goodwill in the world, a Super 12 coach is naturally going to want to hang on to his good players, wherever they're from, for the NPC. For that to happen would negate all the good work the Super 12 has done.

"The Super 12 is also extremely good for club rugby and those who criticised the new structure haven't always been able to see that. When the Super 12 ends, the top 25 or so players are involved in the international part of the season, but 100 or so players go back from the Super 12 to club rugby. That is of enormous benefit to clubs and club players and must remain a feature of the season. All that will stop that happening will be drafted players not returning to their own provinces, or provinces insisting on traditional or 'friendly' provincial matches during the international part of the season. That just interferes with club rugby.

"Rugby has to spread its image, but it also has to spread its image-makers and it can only do that by having the top level of players playing throughout the country and not just in the big centres."

Another concern Lochore has for club rugby is that not enough people are playing the game now. When he was playing for Masterton, the other strong club, a traditional rival in Masterton, was Red Star. Now, the two are combined. "I don't have any great answers, but something has to be done to get more people playing rugby, to get them committed. There is a lack of commitment from New Zealand youth and we have to do something to regain that commitment. There has to be something to attract them to club rugby. Professionalism is not the answer because, in the end, club rugby will be like the base of any other professional sport, it will be amateur. The market determines that and the sooner club officials realise that the better, instead of doing what some clubs in the bigger centres are doing and thinking they can pay their players. It doesn't work like that. All it will succeed in doing is shrinking the very base of the game."

Lochore does not see the plethora of overseas trips for age group rugby teams as the ideal way of regaining a commitment from the young. Too much money is being spent, he thinks, on age group teams going to Australia or Japan or further afield when the money could be better spent on more encompassing development of the same age group in New Zealand. "Too often a lot of money goes into these tours when a young player is 16 or 17 and it's not a sound investment because too many of them are lost to the game when they leave school. The money would be better spent on the new Rugby Academy or on coaches from teams of that level. Hold on to the overseas trips as something special, as a carrot to hold in front of younger players, not as something that should go to them as of right. These teams are full of early maturing kids who you seldom hear of in later years."

In rugby's big years of change, the international calendar is also undergoing profound transformation. The history and traditions of rugby were founded on the tour, the long international tours when the All Blacks seemed to be away for months on end (and sometimes were) and overseas teams seemed to be in New Zealand for months (and sometimes were). The increasing concentration is on shorter and shorter tours and more tests, partly because of money. Tests bring in huge amounts of money, midweek tour matches cost money.

The changing domestic season is also a factor. For years, the highlight of the season for a provincial team was their match against a touring side. The whole focus of the season would be on that match and, if it was won, it instantly became one of the most glorious days in the history of the union. Reunions of old players are founded on such matches. Now, Lochore believes, the rugby tour is becoming more like cricket tours. The internationals are all that matter and the other games are but fillers. County cricket teams, for example, use matches against touring teams as the opportunity to rest their top players and give their second-stringers a chance. Lochore sees that happening in rugby also.

"I consider myself fortunate that I went on one of the last of the long tours. No modern players have had that experience and I think that is a pity."

The introduction of the World Cup in 1987 has been a big factor not just in the shape of rugby tours, but in the approach that all countries, or at least the main ones, now take to international rugby. A possible exception is in Britain where equal attention seems to be given to the Five Nations.

Lochore is a qualified supporter of the World Cup, despite coaching the winning team at the first one and being heavily involved with the team that nearly won the third.

"Right from the outset, I've been against the World Cup being every four years. I think it's too frequent and that six years would be an ideal period between cups. I think four years was chosen because the Olympics are every four years and the soccer World Cup is every four years and no-one at the time thought of anything different.

"But because it's four years, the whole focus is on the World Cup all the time. No sooner has one finished than countries start planning for the next. Everything is geared around the four-year period. Coaches are picked with the next cup in mind and I think four years can be too long for one coach. A six-year gap would allow more of a breathing space, it would allow the ideal coaching span of three years and the greater time between cups would allow countries to look at other aspects of international rugby such as tours. One of the reasons tours are less frequent and shorter is because the World Cup takes out one year in four."

Lochore would not like to see more tests. As a former test player of great distinction, he knows that there is a limit to how many in a season a player can reasonably play, and he knows that already rugby is demanding more of its international players than any other sport does.

"If you equate a test match with a marathon, how many marathon runners do you know who run ten or twelve a year? And you've got to bear in mind all the time that rugby is a full contact sport. In a test match, players are expected to, and do, put their bodies on the line, much, much more than they do in a Super 12 or NPC match. Test matches are extremely physically demanding. It's a bit like going to war – those involved are asked to physically and mentally commit themselves to something that has a toll and to a level that their bodies are not normally subjected to. There is a limit to the number of tests players can properly play in a year and that limit has been reached.

270

"To play any more will have the effect of diminishing the status and worth of test matches and if you do that in rugby, you're blunting the point of the pyramid. It's self-defeating. There are degrees of test matches of course, some countries are harder than others, but the fact is they're still test matches, you're still playing for your country against another."

Referees should benefit more from the new age of rugby. It's no longer good enough for teams when overseas to suffer differing interpretations and differing standards. The Super 12, he says, is an ideal opportunity for referees to gain greater experience by introducing independent referees. Having South Africans in New Zealand or New Zealanders in South Africa will lead to a levelling out of standards and greater consistency – something players appreciate most.

Books such as this normally end with the subject listing his greatest players. Sometimes there's a world team of opponents and sometimes a home team of most valued teammates. Lochore does not want to fall into that trap.

"If I did that," he says, "teams would have to have a lot more than fifteen players."

Those players and coaches who do indulge their whimsy and fantasy, for that is all it can be, especially when players come from different eras, do so usually with the best of motives. It is their tribute to their erstwhile teammates and opponents.

It would be too narrow a brief for Lochore. His tribute is to all his former teammates and opponents, to all who play and have played the game. A lifetime of rugby has brought with it a lifetime of satisfaction and gratitude, and a lot of friends.